To Laura

august
always

best

A Memoir by Jonathan Fisher

wishes
from

Jonathan
x

© Jonathan Fisher 2011. E-mail: jonny.fisher1970@btinternet.com

August Always - Jonathan Fisher

"This is a sad story but also one where, at times, I roared with laughter. It is a story about death but also one about life with all its difficulties, its disasters, its dramas and its delights.

"It is Jonathan's story from his school days, 'hanging around' comic shops, through his time in the Territorial Army, camping in the Mournes, a memorable visit to London for the signing of a copy of much loved comic, his work with local radio and the music scene and far more than his fair share of family tragedies – all culminating in the onset of Addison's Disease.

"Much of the story, and in particular its speech, is written in the language of the comic book or graphic novel... however there are parts of this story that transcend all genres.

"It is in his descriptions of, and his reactions to, the tragedies that occur in his life that the author's talent comes to the fore. It is difficult enough for anyone to deal with such incidents, much more difficult to record them for the public and posterity, but to do so with Jonathan's courage and resolve is quite special. *'August Always'* is worth reading."

Review by Merril Morrow, bookseller Waterstones, Lisburn.

"Truly spectacular. People like Jonathan that are able to get over such hardships are the real heroes."

Irene Schneider, NASA consultant, USA.

I am Jonathan Fisher, *survivor*.

How did I get here?

I was initially formed and developed in my mother's womb. Her name was Emma; my twin David and I shared the same placenta. My father's name was William. I loved my parents very much.

I had a full childhood and subsequent teenage troubles, but when I was twenty-two I suffered an undiagnosed Addisonian Crisis. I was in a coma for three months. The doctors said it would be a mercy to switch off my life-support system, but I moved my little finger whenever my mother asked me – proof of a semblance of life. She was very wise.

Against all odds, I was born again into a mummified state. I was cocooned in a twisted, wasted form, encased in harsh, cruel, snow-white NHS plaster of Paris.

I began the long, slow, hard road to recovery in 1992, a journey that would take me through many institutions and heartaches. I have spent time in the forge and on the anvil, a refining process that has reshaped me both mentally and physically. Progress has been slow at times but consistent nonetheless.

I have been a fighter, a dreamer, a lover and now an author. I am ruthless in my determination to walk again. A living paradox, if you will.

This memoir is just a small sample of my experiences.

And you'd better believe it, baby!

Credits and special thanks to

Photography by Robert Malone
www.malonephotography.co.uk
Graphic Design by Vicki McWhinney at LOV Design
www.lovdesign.com

Many thanks to Bill Jeffrey at the Wordsmiths Forge.
I am very grateful to Jim Burns for the cover painting.
All art created by Jonathan Fisher.

Hardback ISBN: 978-0-9570289-0-6
Paperback ISBN: 978-0-9570289-1-3

Disclaimer: The memoir you are about to read contains some names, places and people whose names have been changed.

Published by PROMETHEUS

For my mother and father,

and

For the brothers Malone, Paul, Robert, Gary

And my friends

The Munnisher and Julian Mullins.

Also for Pat Mills, for his inspiration,

and for everyone who passed through the hallowed portals of 47 Bridge Street, Lisburn…

…this work is respectfully dedicated.

Introduction: I am Jonathan Fisher - Pleased To Meet You
9

Chapter One: It's a Comic Shop, Yeah!
17

Chapter Two: Pat
33

Chapter Three: Shoot to Kill (We Come in Pieces)
53

Chapter Four: Happiness is Dog-shaped
57

Chapter Five: You're in the Army Now!
73

Chapter Six: The Number of the Beast
85

Chapter Seven: 7-7-7 Is My Name
91

Chapter Eight: Born Free
105

Chapter Nine: The Munnisher Cometh
109

Chapter Ten: Glory and Gory Days
119

Chapter Eleven: Titch Fisher
125

Chapter Twelve: Crazy
129

Chapter Thirteen: Unlucky For Some
139

Chapter Fourteen: The Clash of the Titans — Part Two
157

Chapter Fifteen: The Party That Never Ended
163

Chapter Sixteen: That Rainy Day
169

Chapter Seventeen: Death and Glory
201

Chapter Eighteen: My Father
221

Chapter Nineteen: Mummy
231

Chapter Twenty: Volunteering
249

Chapter Twenty-One: Each Day is Like Valentine's Day
255

Chapter Twenty-Two: Logzilla
265

Chapter Twenty-Three: The Ghost of Hallowe'en Town
273

Chapter Twenty-Four: August Always
281

Jonathan, aged 20. Self-portraits

Introduction: I am Jonathan Fisher
– Pleased To Meet You

I remember August. She was my love.

This story begins in my bedroom. My life almost ended there.

In those days, I drew on my bedroom walls like I was a modern-day caveman scribing my art with a religiously zealous, artistic fervour, my trusty black marker pen in hand. I used to dance up and down on my bed, my tongue out, chewing it in concentration as I sketched. My forehead was furrowed deep in thought whilst I focused on my task. Within two nights of feverish drawing, akin to the work of Michelangelo in the Sistine Chapel, lo and behold, my bedroom was covered with various comic characters from *2000 AD*, the Galaxy's greatest comic. Yes!

Unlike my friends, who festooned their own walls with heavy metal posters, I was different. I reflected and copied in minute pointillism style, Judge Dredd, Nemesis the Warlock and Rogue Trooper. These were my heroes and childhood friends. My room contained a bed to sleep on, a crappy portable stereo system, a very Spartan library of around thirty books scattered about my room. I also had a wardrobe with a mirror to admire myself in, and to burst my adolescent blackheads on. There were some beauties on my mirror I can tell you! A cupboard housed my homemade two-inch refractor telescope with its builder's tripod (I was a keen amateur astronomer) and a desk where sat my black and white portable television with my Commodore 64 computer system. Anyway.

It was my daddy — my mummy's "Sweet William", as she would say — who broke the news on that fateful day. My father. He was a royal marine. He was the kind of man who would take off his cap to a lady, and a hearse. He had seen plenty of both. On that particular afternoon, I was sitting on my bed reading a book that I had taken from my bookshelf. It could have been *Dune* by Frank Herbert. I think it was. Yeah, it was. At this point I'm a precocious nineteen-year-old man — an "uncouth youth," as my father would say. Beside me there is a tan-coloured Jack Russell dog curled up in a blanket snoring. Her name is Titch, and my name is Jonathan Fisher. Pleased to meet you.

"Son," he shouted from the bottom of the stairs. "There's a comic shop opening in Lisburn. Your mother was in town and saw the 'opening soon' sign. It's opening tomorrow."

Pausing from reading Frank Herbert's words, I shouted back a simple, "Thanks, Dad!"

Titch pricked her ears up to dad's voice and started to wriggle out of the blanket.

"What's it called?" I yelled in return.

"Your mother said it's called Outer Limits," he hollered back.

Excitedly, I shoved Titch to the side.

"Sorry, doggie, but I have to make a few phone calls!"

I unravelled Titch from her cosy mantle, picked her up from her slumber and set her down on the floor. She shook herself. I put my book away and I bounded down the stairs with Titch trailing close behind.

And, with the scene set, I'm here to tell you a story. It seems that I have been running always. Everywhere. Running from one place to another place. Running from time and out of time. Running from death. Running from life.

I was born along with my elder brother David (we are twins) at The Royal Victoria Hospital in the city of Belfast, here on the planet Earth. At the tender age of seven the family moved. We called it "the big move" to Lisburn. We settled in our wee "house on the prairie", a semi-detached two-storey house, at number 38 Rathvarna Gardens. It was my home, with all the cracks in the ceiling, the cobwebs in the corners and the creaking back gate.

My mother (who was very wise) always described Lisburn as "*Salem's Lot*". (We were fans of the film based on Stephen King's famous vampire novel.) My mother always said that whenever the sun goes down, "the whole town dies."

There is no night-life, you see. And it isn't bias that leads me to say that the only remarkable thing about Lisburn is how boring it is. Oh, sure, nowadays it's becoming some sort of boomtown with cinemas and all that other malarkey — but not in my day. Not in my dimension.

Lisburn was a ghost town to me. So I renamed it "Hallowe'en Town". Well, I could hardly call it "That's your Lot, Salem" as my mother would have said jokingly, or a vengeful lawsuit might ensue. And, secondly, at any given time of year, you will find at least one undead creature roaming through the streets and spires. I will tell you the whole of the Bow Street's unholy mall is rife with zombies, ghouls, spectres and other such beings from the seventh level of Hades. They usually come out at night, with the more adventurous ones emerging out from the twilight to infest the daylight. Some call them "spideys", "chavs", or "hoodies" — take your pick. The others — the more dangerous kind — are called "millies". These are the brides of Beelzebub, evil cockroaches of doom. They come seeking the same things: beer, sex, clothes, and music. You know the sort of thing.

You see, Lisburn is home and host to many things, and offers much. Let me share:

L — *is for lycanthropes — the hairy ones that roam this town*

I — *is for the insane, who mutter, curse and frown*

S — *is for scum, the boy racers who think they're invincible, but they will*

B — *burn in hell, squirming evil dead, despicable*

U — *is for unholy living dead! Zombies are applicable!*

R — *is for roach-ville, there's a lot in this "city"*

N — *is for Nosferatu, who will claim your soul in this town without pity…*

I jest in good humour! If I offended or discriminated against any of these factions, well, tough! Now will you please tell me, is it a hate crime to pick on zombies or Nosferatu? Anyway, the town grew as towns do…

Church of St Patrick's Chapel
Lisburn — approx 4 towers
abandoned when light changed
(The sun disappeared behind

Lisburn Chapel, Chapel Hill, Lisburn

That was until a certain shop opened its doors to Lisburn's youth, acting as some sort of shining beacon of light, alone in the twilight.

Besides the walking undead and the beer-soaking zombies, I refer to my sleepy hollow as I do because I've always loved Hallowe'en all my life. I respected Samhain. That's probably why I was drawn to Lisburn, with "its dark satanic mills" and church spires and its little foibles and faults.

Lisburn has saved my sweet ass on more than one occasion.

This epic journey through my life's events tells of how I became a pirate radio disc jockey, a weekend warrior in the Territorial Army, and was almost arrested for a crime I never committed — a fugitive from the law. It also tells of how I met and shook the hand of an ex-Prime Minister and how I became a rock and roll god, a mountaineer-rescuer, an aspiring artist and a lover to hundreds of women.

Well, okay, maybe not "hundreds" of women, but certainly dozens of them anyway. And by "dozens" I don't necessarily mean in the most precise and literal sense of the word. Perhaps it was only a handful. "Quality, not quantity" is what I always say. My tale also tells of how I died from an illness. That's right, you heard me correctly. I did actually die. This is also the story of how I was brought back to life. For you see, I suffered an undiagnosed full-blown Addisonian Crisis. This tale tells of my on-going struggle from an able-bodied young man to someone who became disabled from Addison's disease and consequently suffered brain injury. *Through sheer will-power I am beginning to learn to walk again.*

This is true.

It all happened to me.

Shall I tell you about my life?

Outer Limits, 47 Bridge St, Lisburn
Left to right: Gary, Paul and Robert Malone

CHAPTER ONE: IT'S A COMIC SHOP, YEAH!

This is the story of a shop — a comic shop, to be more precise. The comic shop in question changed forever the destinies of everyone who entered it. Inhabited by the darkest denizens of Lisburn, where pre-human jokes existed side-by-side with prehistoric clichés: from Goths to anoraks; from mega nerds to metal-heads to skate-boarder punks; from *DC Comics* fans to the fans of *Marvel* and *Black Horse* comics. Every faction of youth came to do homage. The walls of the comic shop themselves told a tale of great heroes, both real and imaginary. An epic of awesome proportions (and then some), a saga of lust, comics, power, comics, intrigue, comics, love, comics, sex, comics — and, just to ensure you have the right idea, more comics! The little shop was just so much more than it looked from the outside: it offered male bonding, metal music, films, chess, Space Crusade and treachery.

And it is I who must tell this tale, for it is I who can. You see, although a story has many sides, each tale is different in the perspective of the observer. I was there.

Right until that day I died.

This is not only the story of a comic shop, but also a tale of a number of men (and a few women), and me, your humble narrator, Jonathan Fisher.

As comic shops go, this one was truly unique. It was a Mecca to Lisburn youth. It came in great ejaculations. It saw and it conquered. Undoubtedly, this store was a destroyer, a corsair, feared by the northern tribes, a usurper amongst comic shops. Essentially, it was the rival of all comic shops in Belfast.

Its four-year mission was to explore strange new worlds, to seek out new life-forms and civilizations…to boldly go where no comic shop had gone before! This was the legend that was to become Outer Limits…

Richard Black, my oldest friend and school pal, was the first to know. The day before, I had phoned him using the house telephone. It was red and had a dial in the front and a pick-up receiver. Excitedly I had told him about the shop opening. We spread the good word. Of course, there were no mobile phones in those days! How quaint and simplistic. Rick had a car. We arranged then to pick up our friends, Paddy and Marty…

Richard and I went to Ballymacash Primary School together. He had brown eyes, mousy-brown hair, and a round face with a smallish chin, complete with John Travolta dimple. We also attended Laurehill High School where we got our O-Levels and, as best friends do at that age, we parted. Richard went on to do his A-Levels at Wallace High School and, as expected, did well. O-Levels were simply a grade in the British education system back then. Graded A, B, C or F

for "failure", or as some of my school chums would say, you are "fucked".

When I left school, I was a little lost and didn't know what to do with myself. They were dark days. I am sure my experience resonates; does anyone know absolutely at eighteen what they want to do for the rest of their working lives?

Well, wandering aimlessly through the possibilities, I tried joining the Forces just as David, my twin brother, had done. David joined the Royal Navy when he left school. He knew exactly what he wanted to do. But I had no direction in life. I was clueless. Hell, I even tried nursing! In these career interviews - interrogations for jobs which, ultimately, were not right for me - I would always get to the examination stage but, after a handshake, goodbye and the slam of the door, it was simply,

"Get on your bike son and fuck you!" as a certain DHS officer once said to me.

"Wham bam, no thank you, Sir!" In those days it was more a case of,

"No experience? No job!" I'll always ask myself how you can ever get experience unless someone gives you a bloody job.

I went down my path. It was then I went to Lisburn Technical College — or The Tech, as it was more infamously known. Big mistake! There I wasted two years in Hell. Lonely, sexually frustrated (so what else was new?), incredibly self-conscious and terribly paranoid to boot. In fact, although I was not aware of it at the time, I was turning into a teenager from Mars!

(During the course of this journey through my memory, I will entertain and regale you, dear reader, with songs of sophistication, great taste and all that other malarkey with "Jay Notes" in the narrative with my explanations — and maybe even some poetry as well. In a story called "The Stupid Gun" Judge Dredd said to his rookie, "Believe me, these culture vultures are the worst!" Anyway.)

[Jay Note: All the songs in this memoir are dedicated to the artists who have inspired me throughout my life. "Thank you for the music and bringing it to me." Honestly.]

"We land in barren fields

On the Arizona plains

We are the angel mutants

The streets for us seduction

Our cause unjust and ancient

In this B-film-born invasion

We need no introduction

For mass annihilation

Inhuman reproduction

We're here for what we want

We want, we need it, we'll take it

We want, we need it, we'll take it, baby

Teenagers from Mars

And we don't care

Teenagers from Mars

And we don't care!"

(Lyrics by Glenn Danzig and The Misfits)

I started my A-Levels at Lisburn Tech, but, without my comrades and their hand-in-hand banter, I found it hopeless. However, I enjoyed Art and I met a few nice people in the second year, including Mr. Peel, my tutor, and Edell Armstrong, Martha Ann and Alison Denvir. These girls were simply a bunch of Goths and Beatniks, but very talented artists in their own way.

The next person in our story is Alan "Paddy" Patrick. He became part of our clan, and was a reliable soul whenever called upon for a favour. Everyone called him "Paddy" for obvious reasons, really. He was the spitting image of Jim Kerr from the band Simple Minds.

I met Paddy through Rick in the fourth year of Laurelhill High School. I remember first noticing that shock of curly hair, the blue eyes and a greasy complexion, and it was Paddy who also had the filthy porno mag under a floorboard in his bedroom! It was vile, honestly. Why a young man at eighteen years old would spank over it is quite beyond me. In the magazine called… well, let's just call it "Golden Oldies," it showed in graphic detail all quite old folks at the age of eighty. "At it." With gusto! And then some! Paddy, if ever asked and questioned about the existence of said literature, would most emphatically deny it, of course. But we all knew about his deviant fetish.

Paddy also went to Wallace High school to do his A-Levels. I should have gone too but, at the time, I was so anti-establishment and such a rebel, or I thought I was, that I just turned away from the lessons and the homework and the living by the schedule. A mistake, I guess, but you learn to live, to survive.

Then we have Marty Møller. I first met Marty in Rick's bedroom. Before we go further, let me first just say: don't worry, we are all hetero! Anyway, Marty asked Rick about his "prog" collection. *[Jay Note: Progs, for the uninitiated, is the abbreviated name of the 2000 AD comic; each "programme" is sequentially numbered.]*

Marty was sifting through Rick's progs; he was looking for a particular issue. It was the beginning of the "Oz / Chopper" saga in Judge Dredd. Rick said to Marty,

"You should ask Jay here, Marty, his knowledge is almost encyclopedic!"

When the word "prog" was mentioned I pricked up my ears, similar to K9, Doctor Who's robotic dog. Chopper was an infamous graffiti artist in Mega-City One, a thorn in the flesh of Judge Dredd. Chopper's wall scrawl was famous on the walls of the Mega-City.

So it was decided. We were going to do an un-American graffiti.

It was a dark, foggy night in Lisburn. The mist shrouded us. I had liberated some brushes and paint from dad's shed. Rick, Paddy and I decided that the squash courts at Laurelhill needed some extra decoration. A lot of extra decoration. In the shadows, with murmurings of praise at each other's handiwork passing between us, with youthful, wanton abandon we went to work with…

CH☺PPER LIVES!

…scrawled in humongous letters and in very bright red paint! It could be seen from the school right across the Prince William Road to the housing estate beyond — and then some!

Marty was, obviously, totally impressed with my knowledge of all things prog-related, and so we found that we had a lot in common. He got me into metal music and a lot of really weird alternative tunes and, quite soon after, we became firm friends. Marty was a real wacky Frood who knew where his towel was. Hoopy! *[Jay Note: the words "Frood" and "Hoopy" are taken from The Hitch Hiker's Guide to the Galaxy by Douglas Adams, what a guy. RIP.]* Marty got his surname, "Møller", from his Danish grandfather. It's not some weird, alien language. Hold that thought for a second. Danish is indeed a weird, alien language. And with his blonde hair and fair features, he was too damn sickeningly handsome for his own good.

Rick Black picked me up from my place round high noon, and we drove along in his blue Toyota motor-car.

The guys often referred to him as "Rick's Taxis." *[Jay Note: We gave Rick that title because we loved the late '70s and early '80s American sitcom, Taxi.]* Let me divert you here

23

and tell you about one evening from the past. "Rick's Taxi" was on call that night for us. As teenagers frequently do, we went for a drink at the Down Royal, a local bar in Lisburn at the time. Paddy, Marty, wee Colin Moore, Rob Hunter (the softy spoken English guy) and myself where crammed into Rick's car. After a session or two in the bar, there was confusion about the pick-up times. The bouncer yelled,

"Taxi for Black! Taxi for Black!" at the top of his voice, meaning, of course, there was another "Black" in the tavern. Singing songs out of tune, they did not care about the pick-up times. Rick bravely volunteered his services. "Rick's Taxi" to the rescue!

Rick said, "Are we ready?" in a drunken tone.

"Don't worry, Jay," he assured me, "I only had a pint!"

That night, he rolled his car right over into a ditch.

"We're all gonna die!" we screamed.

Anyway, moving further along, we picked up Paddy next, then The Møller from his mansion — which requires a bit of an explanation, actually: Marty's house was a fraggin' palace. It had four storeys! *[Jay Note: The word "Frag" is used instead of the words "Forbidden Unknown Carnal Knowledge," otherwise referred to as that ever-so-charming F-word —F.U.C.K.]*

Rick said, "Where should we park this mother-fraggin' machine?" I was sitting in the front seat, looking out for a parking space.

I replied to him with a shrug.

I said, "Wherever's handy, man. What about the wee car park behind Castle Gardens?"

Paddy added, "Aye, that will do." Paddy and Marty where sitting in the back seats.

I pulled down the passenger mirror to admire my handsome visage.

"Mmm, nice," I mused to myself.

Paddy had a huge pimple on his nose, I saw in the reflection.

I turned round to Paddy as I put up the mirror.

"You know, Paddy, you should get a cream for that!" I laughed.

Paddy retorted with the ever-original,

"Frag off, Fisher, you vain git!"

Eventually, Rick parked his car, and we got out of his taxi. Then the "Fantastic Foursome" headed on to OL. *[Jay Note: This phrase became synonymous with the rally call: "Are ya headin' to OL?"]*

In reverence we walked from the car park and we stood outside the soon-to-be sacred walls of the comic shop. I'm pretty sure there was a light in the clouds above us.

The sign above the door said, "OUTER LIMITS — IMPORTERS OF MARVEL, DC, AND INDEPENDENTS." Painted along the sign there were two infamous comic characters: one was Zoo-Loo from *Roachmill*, the other was *Cobalt 90*, an obscure comic character, in my humble opinion. The sign was airbrushed magnificently. *[Jay Note: OL (as it came to be affectionately known by its patrons) was born… nay spawned on Saturday, March 4, 1989. To quote the American president Franklin Delano Roosevelt, "A date which will live in infamy!"]*

Marty was impressed. "Nice sign, man!"

Paddy agreed, echoing everyone's thoughts with his,

"Yeah, cool!"

And without further ado, we entered the shrine.

As we crossed the threshold, I noticed on the inside of the door a poster from *The Princess Bride*, which said, "Abandon Hope, All Ye That Enter Here." A good omen of things to come, no doubt.

The Outer Limits comic shop was the love-child of the three brothers not Grimm, otherwise known as the Malone brothers: there was Gary, the eldest brother; Paul, the middle one; and last, but not least, Robert.

Gary Malone was the tallest of the brothers, and he had a red birthmark on his face. Gary worked for some computers firm in the fair hamlet that is Lisburn, "but not as we know it…"

Robert, the smallest of the Malone tribe, was indeed small in stature but big in — how do I word this? – other departments. He was the Love God of OL. And why, I hear you ask? Well, he was a professional photographer and had no shortage of girls and women in his harem. Enough said.

Paul, the second born, had been drafted into running the comic shop. He had a fine physique and, I suppose I can't blame him, but Paul loved his body. He worked out with weights — and, dare I say, on his girlie friends. Paul previously worked in Wellworths as a workhorse slave, stacking shelves and the like.

The three brothers resembled "pod people clones." Each brother wore glasses and yes, I know you can hear it, someone, somewhere is playing the *Twilight Zone* music!

We found Paul and Robert sitting behind the counter, with Gary just standing. They were all whispering amongst themselves. Remember what I said about the pod people?

The shop itself was quite large compared to other comic shops I've been in, such as Dark Horizons and — Tallywhacker! These rival comic shops were in Belfast and I hated them both; they were too dear and too far to travel to. *[Jay Note: the word "Tallywhacker" derives from the Mojo Nixon song, "Vibrator dependent" and, of course, the afore-mentioned comic shop in Belfast.]* Outer Limits comic shop was a triffid seed waiting to burst into bloom. I looked around. I said to Marty,

"It's got potential." *[Jay Note: a triffid is a face-sucking plant created by the author John Wyndham in his book, Day of the Triffids.]*

Marty nodded his head in agreement. The shop walls were completely bare of posters, artwork and other such comic-related paraphernalia.

Apart from the obligatory *Marvel* filth comics and *DC* dirtballs there was little on the shelves. Surprising! I surmise that they've had a good day or — well, the alternative is too horrible to contemplate!

Eventually, and without much effort, I spotted my prize: on the small Independents shelf there were two copies of *Marshal Law* No. 6. Like Hawkmandude, I swooped down on my prey!

"Oh yes!" *[Jay Note: Marshal Law, the fantastic comic book, is by Pat Mills and Kevin O'Neill   and I made Hawkmandude up right there and then!]*

I continued to scan for the one thing that I believed to be crucial to the life-blood of any comic shop, but no; with confusion and bewilderment I realized, there was none there!

"Where are the progs?" I whispered furiously to my comrades.

Paddy, the diplomat of our group, said,

"Calm down, Jay. There must be a rational explanation for all this."

And then he said, "I certainly hope so!"

I approached the counter optimistically. I walked towards the Malone brood. I placed my purchase on the table. History is made.

"I'll take this one," I said, handing the comic over to Paul.

"Well, boys, there don't seem to be many progs in your shop."

Raising his glasses, Robert asked,

"Progs? What are they?"

Gary replied, "Oh, I know! You're talking about *2000 AD* aren't you?"

"Yes, I am. Do you have any in stock?"

Paul shakes his head. "No, we don't do that in here."

"*You what?*" I was appalled. I took a step back.

"You mean to say, you actually mean to tell me, that you don't do *2000 AD?*" In a rage, stepping forward again, I slammed my right fist on the table top. I said, "And what sort of comic shop is this anyway? Cool sign though. Which one of you guys did it?"

"I did." Paul freely admitted.

"It's a damn fine sign!" I offered my hand in friendship to Paul. We shook hands. Paul had a firm, manly hand.

"I am Jonathan Fisher."

"Paul. Paul Malone. These are my brothers, Robert and Gary."

They all shook hands with me.

"These are my good friends: Rick Black, Alan Patrick and Marty Møller." Again, they shook hands in turn.

When the ice was broken, the conversation was free and easy all that Saturday in spring. In fact, it seemed that time had stopped for a little while, and all of us felt something: a bond. It sounds corny, I know, and of course it's a cliché, but it's true. It was like a meeting of minds and more. It was like a fraternity coming together for the first time. A true band of brothers.

"How was your first day, Robert?" Marty asked.

"Oh," Robert replied, as he added the total from the book and the till, "around two hundred and fifty pounds." He smiled, bobbing up and down.

Rick whistled appreciatively.

"Well, guys! So, what do you reckon?" I asked.

"I bought a copy of *Roachmill*. What about you, Paddy?" added Marty.

"Well, I kinda got an issue of *Love and Rockets*, kinda thing." That was Paddy's fixation. He said those two words in almost every sentence he spoke. *[Jay Note: Roachmill was created by the duo Hedden and McWeeney, a great comic book. And Love and Rockets was produced by the Hernandez brothers.]*

"And you, Rick?" I said.

"I bought the other *Marshal Law.*" he replied.

Soon, it was time to go. We made our farewells, and we helped the lads put the grilles onto the shop window.

"Are we ready?" Rick asked.

On the way home, everyone agreed that Outer Limits must be the finest, grooviest place in the entire universe. How were we to know about the doom that would eventually destroy us all?

But that was to come in the future, and then life was all about the "here and now." And so we lived it.

In Outer Limits
Paul Malone and Bones the Surfing Skeleton

CHAPTER TWO: PAT

The next few days at the shop were quite eventful. After a heavy weekend of debauchery, the Malones re-opened the store on Tuesday and I met my arch nemesis — Aynat Bubezleeb — the absolute evil spawn of the devil; most importantly none must ever, ever spell or even speak her name forwards — just in case thou shalt suffer the agony of the seventh level of hell, and then some! *[Jay Note: her name was a play on words, and if you did speak her real name aloud you would suffer great torment. I thought her name up after watching the dancing dwarf scene in Twin Peaks.]*

Well, anyway, as I was saying, Aynat, to my mind, looked like a vicious, ginger harpy. I suppose some might say she had a great body. I know some of the guys thought so, including Paul who was going out with her at the time, and Alan McColonicIrrigation *[Jay Note: we'll have the dubious honour of meeting this individual a little later, dear reader, so be patient.]* who lusted after her. Me? Well, let's just say I was tempted; I was, after all, Virgo Intacto at that time! However, irrespective of her figure, looks or other enticing attributes, the truth remained that she had an absolutely grim demeanour — and that was only her nose!

I came through the door of the comic shop — I bounded through it, almost taking the door off its hinges. I was at the infamous Lisburn Tech, and I ran down the hill to get out of that piss-hole. I found, sitting on the "con," *[Jay Note: the "con" is Captain Kirk's chair.]* the aforementioned Aynat! She was wearing a Hunterhouse school uniform, a school in Belfast for girls only, twinned with St. Trinian's; her skirt was shortened, showing her legs. Enough for a good eyeful I suppose. I'm sure Paul knew. Paul had a good eye, an eye for the ladies. A roving eye. *Aye.* But, anyway, enough of this character assassination — on with the story!

"Where's Paul?" I asked the creature. I panted out of breath.

An awkward silence passed between us.

A woman? In a comic shop? And not only in a comic shop, but sitting *on the seat of power?* Who would countenance such a thing?

Aynat replied in her banshee voice,

"Pa-ul! You've a visitor!"

Paul appeared from the back door of the shop.

"Oh, sorry, Jonathan, I was in the dunny!"

"That's okay, man! I hope you washed your hands!"

I don't think I've mentioned this before, but all of the Malones have Australian accents, though Paul's is much stronger. Although not Australian, during their formative years they went to school in Oz, "the land down under, can't you hear the thunder, you'd better run, you'd better take cover." Anyway.

"Err, umm, Paul, is this your girlfriend?" I asked disbelievingly, nodding over to Aynat.

The way I said "your" must have given Aynat cause to take offence. Maybe she thought I called her another word, one rhyming with "your" but, either way, Paul introduced me and I shook her hand. It was kind of limp.

Possibly going off on a bit of a tangent here, but I think there are three kinds of handshake on this Earth. The first must be the "we are equals" handshake, which may comprise some form of locking, which includes the thumbs and palms coming together in unison, if you understand my meaning. The second is what I tend to describe as the "clergy" handshake, which was usually administered by the Reverend George Irwin — our family's Minister. As I sit telling this tale, for the life of me, I think I have only once had the "equal" shake. On other occasions, it's the clergy, a bone-crushing shake, delivered by the one and only Rev. And then there is the third, which is the "I don't want to know you and you're not my friend" handshake, most often used by women. I know that when the last statement will be read, some people may think I'm a sexist pig but that's not true, you know. Okay, it's partly true; okay, it's true. But, whether true or not, that's the sort of shake Aynat gave me: a limp, shallow greeting of sorts. The kind that told us both we'd never be more than a recognised face to one another. *[Jay Note: you will probably notice during this story that I use little pastiches and quips, for example, "That's true you know, that's partly true you know, and okay it's true." This is a quote from Marshal Law created by Pat Mills and Kevin O'Neill. All hail Pat Mills, comic creator supreme!]*

From that first day and forever onwards, Aynat and I never saw eye to eye.

Well, that might not be strictly right. There was the time I mooned at her and generously gave her a view of my inner eye — but that's another story to come!

Well, after a few cigarettes (she was a chain smoker, to add to her most heinous crimes, and an underage drinker and chronic alcoholic to boot), Aynat took her leave.

I was at the back of the shop, trying to read while all the mushy stuff was going on.

"Praise the holy prophet, Zarquon, she's gone!" I muttered under my breath finally. *[Jay Note: The Holy Prophet Zarquon was yet another character from The Hitch Hiker's Guide to the Galaxy by Douglas Adams — the same genius, RIP — and all hail Zarquon.]*

I sat down on the small stool beside the "con" and then plied Paul with the progs I had in my blue binders. I showed him *Nemesis,* by my comic book creator idol, Pat Mills, and Kevin O'Neill, and then *Slaine,* with Pat and Mike McMahon. He was in awe. He flicked through the pages, the holy parchments. Similar to a monk holding *The Book of Kells,* in reverence.

"I didn't know there was such good stuff in these progs, Jonathan," said Paul, trying to get his mouth around the word "prog." It was a new word for Paul to master, and a new world to conquer.

"You see! Paul, my friend, you have taken the first step on the long road to enlightenment! Oh and call me Jay, all my other friends do!"

"Well, thank you, Jay!"

"Say, Paul, did I tell you about the time I met Pat Mills at Tallywhacker, the so-called *Crisis* tour?"

Paul was surprised. "Were you there, man? Me and Gary were there too!"

"Frag right! He has dubbed me 'The Heckler from Belfast', man! Allow me to explain. Right, the journey began at my house. I read about this tour in that *Crisis* crap. I decided to go down and meet the guy. The day of the signing came along, and I walked — or rather ran — down the road to catch the train to Belfast. I was prepared. I had with me my *Cursed Earth* albums, my *Marshal Laws* and, of course, the first appearance of *Slaine* all for him to sign." *[Jay Note: Slaine is a Celtic barbarian, created by Pat and Angie Mills, for the Galaxy's greatest comic, 2000 AD, all hail Tharg the Mighty, alien editor supreme!]*

"Anyway, I got down to Tallywhacker. Inside there was quite a large crowd waiting for the lads. Pat Mills was sitting on the left side of the table, and in the middle there was John Smythe, the self-confessed homosexual. I stayed well clear of him, let me tell you. Some people think that I'm homophobic, and I'll tell you, Paul, that's very true, you know.

"Anyway, on the right side of the table, was Jim Baikie, the self-confessed Orkney Islander. (I joke!) Above and about them was this entire *Crisis* malarkey, banners that were put up by the Tallywhacker crowd, and I thought to myself, what a load of old cobblers! *[Jay Note: The Crisis comic was created by Pat Mills — and it really was a load of cobblers!]*

"Pat Mills is a tall, thin kind of guy. He wore black leather trousers — skin-tight, I might add! — and he smoked small, thin cigars, tsk, tsk. In fact, he looked a bit like your man Ray Alan; you know that guy with that drunken dummy, Lord Charles, yeah?"

"The one with the monocle?" Paul asked.

"The very same. Anyway, I stood in the queue for Pat. He was easily the most popular guy there and quite soon after, it was my turn to set my stuff down on the table for him to sign. My throat was dry. I was excited. I shook his hand — what a grip, man! I proceeded to introduce myself:

"'Hello there, Pat Mills! My name is Jonathan Fisher, and I am your Number One fan!' A little like Kathy Bates in Stephen King's *Misery!* I was also his Number One critic — but he didn't need to know that, yet! Just as Oliver Hardy would have acted in disgust at Stanley Laurel's antics, I sighed and raised my eyebrows. Anyway, I think it's fair to say that Pat was a little taken aback. He didn't know how to take me at first. People seldom do, Paul. Like my sense of humour, I mean. But when they do, they can see that I'm a liberal, easygoing kind of guy. And that's true." *[Jay Note: I am a fan of the legendary duo, Laurel and Hardy. They were comedy myths in movies in early 1930s America.]*

"So did you guys talk?" Paul asked me.

"Well, I discussed Pat's career; his high points, his low points — especially the low points! This was just a bit of harmless banter between two intellectuals. And all the while he put his scrawl on the various comics that were presented to him. I stood at Pat's shoulder, looking out at the seething crowds of goths, metal heads, cheese rangers and anoraks. Surprisingly, actually, Pat and I got along quite well, which is probably because, at the time, it seemed that I was the only one speaking to the man. However, more and more people joined in with our conversations towards the end of the afternoon."

"'So, Pat, was that your wife that co-created *Slaine* with you?' I asked.

"'Yes, it was,' he responded whilst signing a few issues of *Crisis.*

"'Err, I think You-ko is a great character, a bit like Ro-Jaws, in fact.' I said, trying to get the conversation going a bit."

[Jay Note: Ukko is Slaine's sidekick, and Ro-Jaws and Hammerstein are from the A.B.C. (Atomic, Bacterial, Chemical) Warriors, created by Pat Mills from the Galaxy's greatest comic, 2000 AD, all hail Tharg the Mighty, alien editor supreme!]

"'You-ko?' he asked questionably. 'I've always called him Uk-oh, that's interesting. I'll have to make a note of your colloquialism!' And he looked up at me and said, 'Where's your issues, then?'

"'Well,' I said shrewdly, 'I left them in the house because they're currently acting as a load of "masturbatory material hornswoggle", especially *The Statesmen* rubbish!' This last bit was aside to John Smythe. He heard it."

[Jay Note: The New Statesmen was created by John Smythe and the Orkney Islander. Yes, it was masturbatory material hornswoggle — and that's being generous!]

"'Now, hold on there, Jonathan — justify yourself. You can't just make broad, sweeping statements like that!' he told me.

"'No? Watch me!' And I let rip on him — although I didn't fart, but I was sorely tempted to. Instead, however, I said, 'Well, Pat, you know as well as I do, it's gonna fold into comic oblivion! For a start, it's far too pricey. For another thing, the content! Homosexual superheroes with a *Watchmen* slant — what a complete rip-off! And there's *Troubled Souls*! Please!' I rolled my eyes in disgust before continuing on with my rant. 'I don't know where those two jerks got their story and material from, Pat, you Sassenach, but I've lived in Belfast for most of my life and people simply don't do that sort of thing over here! And, another point, there's that tripe you created — *Third World War!* Okay, it made me think, I admit…'

[Jay Note: Watchmen, the comic book bible, was created by Alan "we were not worthy" Moore and the mighty Dave Gibbons. Troubled Souls was created by Garth Ennis and John McCrea, who both worked for the evil anti-opposite to Outer Limits comic shop, "Dark Whorizons."]

"Pat cut in at this point. 'But, Jonathan.' He came closer. 'The whole philosophy of *Crisis* is that it's meant to make you think…'

"'Yeah, aye, well, as you say, but I reckon your best stuff was in the progs,' I said, trying to wean him off the subject. 'For instance, your early stuff in *2000 AD* was simply fantastic!' I added with real enthusiasm.

"Pat took notice of this — he sat upright and treated himself to a cigar.

"While Pat busied himself, I continued.

"'You see, *Flesh* I really enjoyed, me being into dinosaurs at that time.' I waved my hand to blow the smoke away, coughed and said,

"'Here, Pat, didn't you write the Judge Dredd story about the three hoods who rob a tobacco store and kill the owner? After the hoods leave and JD is called in to investigate the crime, there is a spate of robberies throughout the Mega-City One, same MO, yeah? Well, when the next crime occurs, the Judge is waiting for them at the store. The Judge is at the back of the store, in the shadows, posing as a wooden Indian, and so when the lawbreakers complain to the shopkeeper about the position of the Indian, they light up on JD! Now, the Judge says,

"'"You struck the Law! Now the Law strikes you!" And he proceeds to kick some ass!

"'One perp escapes, however, and he's waiting outside in his pod-car to gun down Dredd as he comes out the door, but Dredd flies out of the window, smashing it in the process, on his Lawmaster and says,

""'Dead men use doors, live ones use the window!'' or some other such malarkey! Anyway, at this point the guy craps himself and says,

""'I gotta get outta here!'' And he does — but not for long: Dredd, you see, uses the bike cannon on him and blows the pod sky-high! But then it appears that the punk — let's call him Smoky — survived! Well, Smoky tries to make a run for it but, as he is a smoker, he can't run all that fast or even that far, and so Dredd catches him up and uses his huge rifle, the Lawrod, and blows Smoky away!'"

[Jay Note: a 'perp' is a perpetrator of a crime.]

"I took a breather and looked from face to face, checking that everyone was still interested. They were.

"'Sliding down the wall is the remains of the Lawbreaker. Turning round, Dredd, ever so coolly blows the smoke from the barrel of his weapon, and then the one and only Judge says,

""'Justice Department health warning: Smoking can kill you!'"

"'So, Jonathan, is there a point to your story or what?' Pat breathed his smoke on me again. 'We're all addicted to something: sex, love, whatever,' he shrugged. What are *you* addicted to? What do you do? What's in it for you, Jonathan?'

"'Me? I'm in it for the energy!' I shouted, both fists clenched and raised over my head. I eventually set them down and said,

"'That must be one of my favourite quotes from *Marshal Law*, Pat; they say imitation is the sincerest form of flattery.'

"Pat nodded his head.

"'To answer your first question, I am addicted to adrenaline and Life. As Slaine once said,

"''I'm not afraid of death, but I like living better." Nothing else — I don't even drink alcohol.'

"'Very commendable,' Pat sneered sarcastically.

"'Well, at least I'm not a hypocrite!' I waved a critical finger at him. 'I thought you had more sense — you being my Number One comic-creator and all. I sort of thought that, because of that anti-smoking story you wrote in the Prog, that you would be totally against smoking. Obviously not.'

"'Okay, okay, I'll put the fraggin' thing out! There! Satisfied? Jesus, you don't half go on!'

"'Thank you for your co-operation, Citizen!'"

At this point, I turned my attention to Paul.

"True to form, Paul, he didn't smoke in my presence again."

"What else did you say?"

"Allow me to continue."

I paused.

"'As I was saying, Pat, I'm a student at Lisburn Tech where I try to study Art and Design. I went to school at Laurelhill High School before that. Where did you go to school, Pat?'

"He shuddered at the thought of his old school, and then said with venomous undertones,

"'I went to a very strict Catholic boarding school in England. The monks in there were a vicious, evil bunch of bastards!'

"I laughed at this but he cut me down.

"'It wasn't funny, Jonathan! Those fraggers nearly ruined my bloody life! It's true what they say: "Give me a child and I'll shape him into anything" — Tomas De Torquemada.'

"'I thought Adolph Shicklgruber (Hitler) said that in *Mein Kampf*, Pat?

"'No, no,' he said, shaking his head. 'It was probably Torquemada. Anyway, about this school: it only contrived to turn me into a warped and sick monkey-slapping individual. My only friend in that hell-hole was Kevin O'Neill; as you may be aware, Kevin designed the look of *2000 AD* and Tharg. He's sicker and even more depraved and twisted than I'll ever be! In fact, when we work together as a team, we try to out-do each other. Kevin surpassed my wildest imaginations every time! This was a friendly competition between us. The grosser and more disgusting my script was, Kevin would try to out-do me with his artwork. He was the only artist whose work was banned in America for a story he did.'"

[Jay Note: The Comic Code of America banned Kevin's issue of the Green Lantern because he depicted a character being crucified; this particular issue was written by Alan Moore.]

"'I knew that,' I said with great conviction. 'Tell me about *Nemesis* Book One. That was a great story. Good art! But Book Two was a bit dodgy. Jesus Redondo did the art on that one. A bit of a let-down and a bit sketchy.'

"'Yes,' Pat agreed. He took a long breath in. He sighed. 'His work on that story was a touch disappointing. I suppose you didn't like Mike McMahon's work on *Slaine,* either, Jonathan?'

"'Hey! Do bears crap in the woods, Pat?" I exclaimed. 'Course I did! The *Shoggey Beast* is a true classic, as is *Sky Chariots*!'

"At this point, an anorak interloped into our conversation and said,

"'Excuse me, Mr Mills, sir, but how much do you get paid per graphic novel?'

"'Not enough,' was his sharp reply. He looked away into the distance.

"'Is that right?' I said, my eyes wide open. 'Come off it, Pat! You must have loads of money, right?'

"'Wrong,' he turned and met my gaze. He growled angrily.

"'Do you realise how much we creators are paid by Titan books?' He picked up my graphic novels and waved them in my face for a moment.

"'A measly five per cent! That's why we created *Crisis,* so that the creators could get credit for their creations!'

"'That seems most unfair, but I thought Tharg was…'

"He interrupted me with a burst of laughter.

"'Oh, you don't believe in Tharg, do you? I created Tharg — he was our bastard lovechild. Kevin was the father and I was his mother! I wrote all of his stories.'

"'All of his stories?' I queried. 'Even the photo strips?'

"And it was then that something occurred to me. It was bubbling up, overwhelming me — I just had to tell him this!

"'I noticed you did a photo strip in one of the summer specials, *Nemesis the Photo Story*. Err, that was a bit crap, wasn't it, Pat?'

"He put his head down and looked away, trying in vain to ignore this.

"However, I went on without mercy, in for the kill. I started laughing! I said, 'Oh, yes! I can see it now! What an abomination! What an obscenity that was, Pat! Where did you get those people from and those props? What was Torque like?' I was close to falling about on the ground in laughter! 'It was just like one of those love stories you see in girly magazines such as *Just 17* and *Bunty* for instance. And *The New Eagle* comic, of course, which was notorious for that sort of thing!'"

[Jay Note: Nemesis the Photo Story was an utter travesty. Enough said!]

"He looked at me with great menace, his face beginning to turn red. Oh-oh, I thought to myself, I've struck a chord here!

"'Look,' he snarled, 'I don't want to talk about it, okay?' He looked fit to burst!"

Paul was riveted.

"'Alright, alright! Sheesh! Keep your hair on!' and I said under my breath, "'Touchy! Very touchy!'

"Right at that moment, Marty and Alan McColonicIrrigation appeared, looking right out of place in their Wallace High School uniforms. That is to say they stood out —big time! Everyone stared at them. There was silence. Someone spoke to me — or should I say something grunted. It was McColonicIrrigation.

"'Err, hi there, Jay. What's happening?' he squeaked.

"Paul, I think I should describe Alan McColonicIrrigation for you, — just in case he comes into Outer Limits. He's bound to. Simply put, I just don't like the guy. Why, Paul? Well, I don't quite know, man. He just rubs me up the wrong way. He knows exactly how to rile me — and boy he does! Besides, he looks like a pink, fat rat. In fact, all his school chums call him 'Pinky!'

"But where were we, man? Oh, yes, we were in Tallywhackers. Let me proceed.

"'Meeting Pat Mills is what's happening here, Alan!' I said.

"'Men, meet the one, the only, Pat Mills!' I proffered them up to the warlock himself and told them to shake his magnificent paw, which they did, of course.

"They both had *Marshal Law* and *Crisis* mags for him to stamp his signature on.

"We chatted away; that is, until I noticed the clock on the wall: it read a quarter to five.

"It was time for us to go.

"'Listen, Pat, it's been… enlightening and fun. We had a marvellous time. Oh, one last thing!' I rushed over and bought a copy of *Crisis* and rushed back and said, 'Here, put your mark on this one, Pat! It's just for the old collection, you understand?'

"'Why, you two-faced son of a gun! Okay, I'll sign it for you, but this is the last thing. My hand is growing weary.'

"We both shook hands. He tried to crush my hand   he tried to give me the Clergy shake, but I wasn't having any of that. I squeezed tighter. He looked me in the eye. Then I said,

"'As we say in our country,

"""May the road rise to meet you,*

May the wind be always at your back,

The sun shine warm upon your face,

The rains fall soft upon your fields

And until we meet again

May God hold you in the hollow of his hand."""

"Then I added, '*Nemesis the Photo Story!*'

"We disengaged.

"'You bastard!' he moaned back.

"But there was a last, final thing to say.

"'Live long and prosper!' I called out. And then, with a wave of my mighty hand, we were gone from that place, my comrades and I, into the wilderness in search of public transportation.

"We got the train home."

"What a laugh, man!" Paul said.

I had to agree.

We both laughed.

Just at that minute, a school juvenile came bouncing through the door of the shop. He was wearing the distinctive green of a Friends school uniform — and he didn't shut the bloody door! That was his first mistake. You see, the guys didn't have any money for heating at the time. Besides, it was standard OL protocol — and polite!

I reached over and slammed the door shut. Paul and I looked at the guy and stared with our mouths wide open in utter amazement.

The guy's hair was a huge Afro — an African hairstyle type of thing. But his hair was ginger! Dun dun dah!

"Hey you, Curly, were you born in a field?" I asked, tactfully.

Curly mumbled an apology and turned to the corner that housed the *DC Comics* and Independents.

Mysteriously, and without any sort of warning, out of the void that is the time/space continuum, from another dimension came Frank Zappa! Would you believe it?

"Wow!" said Curly and Paul in unison.

[Jay Note: Frank Zappa appeared from time to time at the shop as little Zebedee from The Magic Roundabout. He would play a song, buy a comic, and play a rift on Paul's guitar, hot curly weenie, weenie, weenie!]

As quickly as he appeared, the guru vanished into the void. Back to reality.

"I'm sorry, Curly. Let's shake."

He looked at me oddly. "O-kay," he said hesitantly, "but the name's Gavin, actually."

"Good, man!" He had a reasonable shake. "Well, 'Gavin Actually,' welcome to our shop — or I should say your shop, Paul," I added to Paul, just in case he thought Curly would get the wrong idea.

"So what can we do you for, Mr Actually, exactly?" I said in a friendly shopkeeper kind of way.

"Hardy har har!" Gavin replied, with a great deal of sarcasm, which was to become his whole trademark for his entire life.

Gavin Curly Hughes

"My surname is Hughes, okay?"

"Okay, okay! Keep your hair on! Oh, excuse me, I appear to have made a joke about your curly hair again! I'm sooo sorry!"

This banter could have gone on all day — well, it did. We discovered that Gavin "Hot Curly Weenie" Hughes was a Goth and had a brother called Gary, for his sins.

"I bet you're the kind of sad bastard that reads *Sandman*," I said, leaning my back on the wall whilst looking out of the window. It had started to rain.

"As a matter of fact, I am — and proud of it! But I also read *2000 AD* and *Swamp Thing*."

"That, my friend," I said with great relief, "is the only reason I've allowed you to live. For if it is not written by the holy jockstrap of Robert E. Howard you'll pay for that hell-spawn!"

Then there was a clap of thunder and, of course, a few bolts of lightning (or should that be the other way round?). Anyway, a dark figure then appeared out of the darkness! It came from beyond the stars — or Upper Ballinderry!

Paul Andrews

"Oh, hi there, Paul," Gavin said. "Guys, this is Paul Andrews."

Paul Andrews had the same uniform as Gavin, and when he stepped into the light he was not as foreboding as he initially seemed. Little were we to know about his satanic powers! At that time, his appearance was, well, bearable to behold — for a Beelzebub! He had a big round moon of a face, on which protruded bulging brown eyes; he had a pug nose and spoke with a soft lisp.

"Greetingths, Friendsth. Do you guyths stockth any Nemesisth the Warlocksth comicth?"

Okay, his lisp was not all that well pronounced; I am exaggerating. So, for sanity's sake, we are switching to Paul Andrews in normal speech sync mode!

"What a strange coincidence," I said, "for with great fortune, I just happen to have on my person a wide selection of *Nemesis* comics that you might want to read!"

I turned my attention to Paul Malone.

"There it is. Pure proof, if proof was needed, in the power of the progs."

Well, to end the day, the sun started to come out of the clouds. Mr Sunshine began to evaporate the rain from the pavements of Lisburn. Eventually it was twenty-five past five in the afternoon. It was time to leave. But there was one last duty to perform.

"Would you help me on with the window grilles, Jay?" Paul asked.

"No worries. Listen," I grunted whilst lifting a mighty grille. "Would you mind if me and Marty and Rick come and visit you some night? You all live in Llewellyn Avenue, don't you?"

"Sure! Why not?"

When all three window grilles were in place, I said farewell to Paul. We walked in opposite directions — he went down the hill, and I went up it.

Chapter Three: Shoot To Kill (We Come In Pieces)

At that time in my life, I was as fit as the proverbial fiddle. I was nineteen — and, like all nineteen year-olds, I was immortal: I had my health, I was able-bodied, and had the sex drive and appetite of a Tyrannosaurus Rex. Ahhh, yes, life was good.

Not many adolescents would voice this but, at the time, family life was also pretty good, though when I say "good" I mean we got along. Don't get me wrong; we weren't quite the Waltons or the Ingalls — but who is, really? We had our problems but we worked through them.

But then the excrement, so to speak, started to hit the fan when my dad, William, lost his job. He was "made redundant". What a horrible, bloody awful phrase that is. He never deserved that. Throughout his entire life my dad was a very active man. When he was a young man he joined The Royal Marines and became a Commando. He fought for King and Country in Malaysia, in Borneo and in the Suez Canal conflict. I always wondered what it would be like to actually *kill* someone, but I never asked him and he didn't say, so we left it at that. I suspect he killed a few hundred men during his time in the line of duty.

In fact, my dad was in three Great War films of that era (albeit as an extra!) One was called *The Cockle Shell Heroes*. The others I can't remember at this time.

My dad's exploits in The Marines inspired my twin David and me to trace his footsteps. Well, at least in some way. When Dave left school at seventeen, he joined The Royal Navy. A wee bit later — okay, sometime later — I also tried to "join up."

I gave the news to Paul that fateful day.

"Paul, me old china," I said with great sadness, "I must regretfully inform you that I have to do service for my Queen and country — well, for the next three weeks or so."

"Why?" Paul asked, looking surprised.

"Because I have … I have to…" I stammered and gulped. "I have to join the TA! It's a pride thing," I continued. "You see, Paul, I come from a long line of warriors, men at arms, call them what you will. My dad was a Marine, so was my uncle David and, as you know, my twin David is in The Navy. Logically, I have to join The Territorial Army."

At this point, we all quoted that famous line from *The Young Ones* TV comedy show where Neil the Hippie says,

"Join the TA. You - can - have -a- gun - if- you - want - one."

When the laughter died down, Paul spoke. He said in a soft voice,

"I was in the army, once." He hugged Aynat. *She* was there too.

Marty, who was also in the room with us and heard our conversation, sat down on one of the stools (stools were in short supply) and said to Paul,

"What did you do? Leave?"

Paul looked sad. "I had to buy myself out, guys. I couldn't keep a straight face. I just kept on laughing at The Sergeant!" He gave a wry smile but, in all honesty, I think that had something to do with whatever Aynat did to him underneath the counter, which we, thankfully, couldn't see.

I said goodbye to Marty, Paul and the shop. I was about to embark on the experience of a lifetime — and then some!

My Grand
Father.
1 have.
HB

55

My Father, by Jonathan

Titch Fisher, by Jonathan

CHAPTER FOUR: HAPPINESS IS DOG-SHAPED

The next few chapters, dear reader, will not be for those with a nervous disposition. Warning: this is for added realism and will involve various inflections on the F-word, the W-word, the S-word, etc.! In fact, it will be downright fornicating vulgar!

If Outer Limits was heaven on Earth, The TA building in Lisburn was its evil and satanic opposite. The denizens inhabiting that place were a mixed bunch of… what's the word? … wankers, yes, that's the word. That seems to be quite an accurate way of describing the numb-nuts running the entire operation.

I chummed around with my old friend Ivan McGalway — he went to Laurelhill High School. We were class mates together. To my mind, he looks a bit like Gil Favour, trail boss, out of *Rawhide* — and he's one of these bigoted "Super Prods." But I liked him. He was a good laugh. He was another Lisburn Tech lad, another drop-out. I was very pleased to see him there.

However, there were quite a few other interesting characters in evidence. These comprised the rest of my cadre, which included the biggest bunch of drunks, loudmouths, and assorted gung-ho ass-holes ever to have walked this planet.

And then there was me. And Ivan, of course.

First of all, there was Finnley McCesspit; everyone called him "Finn." This guy looked like a hyena, smelled like a hyena and laughed like a hyena. Yes, to all intents and purposes Finn was a hyena. He worked in Frasier's — the High-street clothing store in Lisburn — as a sales rep. Then came Tom O'Plum the Plumber. This guy had *three* nipples! I renamed him "Scaramanga", you know *The Man With The Golden Gun* from James Bond? *[Jay Note: Bond, James Bond was created by Ian Fleming. "Dum di-di dum dum, da da da, DAA DAA!" That's my impression of the James Bond theme tune.]* Next came Brian who was, well, let's just say he was the opposite of Ivan. Okay, he was a catholic and, surprisingly, they got on quite well. Then there was big Ginge, James and Conrad: these boys were from "Pordydown." Next was wee George and Tash with a mousy moustache, which he clearly thought did him a favour. (It didn't). And it was all of us together who formed our Platoon of Doom, our Army of Darkness, our Legion of the Damned, and our Cadre of Crap! And this was my first exposure to the total insanity that is War and then some!

Before basic training began, we had to travel up north to Camp Milligan — which was more like Camp O'Helligan. It was scary, and it was cold as a witch's tit!

When we got out of the truck, it was time to stretch our legs and, for some of the lads, a quick cigarette. Then, the previously unmentioned Corporal O'Tool (who had come along with us for the ride) showed us to our billets. We were then issued with one smelly, and I do mean smelly, sleeping bag; this sucker really hummed.

I was glad to bed down for the night. However, some of the other men went to the Naffy for beer.

That night must rank amongst one of the worst of my entire life. Being an army camp, it had a large drinking establishment, just like the TA in Lisburn, and when it went dark, the orgy of drinking, cursing and general mayhem ensued.

Ivan, of course, enjoyed himself, as did the rest of the men. I didn't. When I see people taking drugs of any description I tend to distance myself from them and keep my head down, out of their way, especially strangers.

"People are strange when you're a stranger

Faces look ugly when you're alone

Women seem wicked when you're unwanted

Streets are uneven when you're down

When you're strange

Faces come out of the rain

When you're strange

No one remembers your name

When you're strange

When you're strange

When you're straaaaange!"

(Song lyrics by The Doors)

Well, I tried to get some sleep and bunkered down for the night but it was completely impossible, what with the rave music some corporal was playing and the swearing, which was utterly out of this world, not to mention the sound of beer cans being thrown at the opposite wall by the weekend warriors. To add insult to injury, some of those cans were a bit on the full side, making for a nice unwanted spray of beer, which drenched the floor and the walls, laying its stickiness out for the morning. To make the point that bit clearer, and without even a hint of exaggeration, by the morning there were at least five hundred beer cans piled up against the dormitory wall. The bottom line: they were simply savages; a monkey's tea party has more decorum!

The morning came painfully slowly; it must have been around three when they dozed off. Finally, I thought to myself, relieved, time for a bit of shut-eye. But then, just one short, teasing hour later, the horror began anew!

Despite being beyond exhausted, I was, however, glad to get up out of that pit. Blurry-eyed and still yawning, I stumbled into the washroom with most of my cohorts, including Finn and Ivan, for a quick shave and teeth-brush. It was then, right there in the washroom, that I was given my nickname by that laughing Dingo, Finn.

"Hey, there, Colgate! How's about ye?" He slapped my naked back.

"Piss off, you little runt!" was my foamy-mouthed reply. I was still brushing my teeth and I recoiled in anger, both at the remark and his slap. It was freezing in the washroom and I was in no mood for his antics that early in the morning. Thanks to his friends, I'd had a hellish night.

The moon was out on the parade ground, casting long, pale blue shadows. When parade was called, some of us warmed up in the cold frosty air, stretching our muscles, breath going in cold and streaming out fire and steam. The moon was waning into its last quarter and the sky was full of stars; it gave me hope for the day ahead.

Enough daydreaming, I thought to myself. There's that bloody Corporal!

"Okay, men, it's time for your *BFT.! Fall out! Quick march! Left, right!!*" The man bellowed every word.

The basic fitness test was just a simple five-kilometer run around the camp. I was really eager to get into it; I had been training for weeks in the hills close to my home back in Lisburn. I found the run quite stimulating despite the biting wind that slowed me down a bit and made my eyes water in the wind. I pitied those fat buggers with beer bellies, all of them wobbling along on their last legs, and the smokers who were hacking and coughing their lungs out.

During our run, the stars faded away. Gradually, the sun began to rise and it warmed our journey.

Eventually, the end was in sight, and, none too soon for the cardiac-arrest patients who were like beached whales when they flopped to the ground after their ordeal. After a while, they eventually stopped moaning, groaning and swearing.

They finished last, of course and, suffice to say, Corporal O'Tool was not pleased. Like he could talk — he followed in a Land Rover, the total dick-wad.

Quite soon after, it was time for breakfast in the mess hall. I'll say something good for the TA; the food wasn't that bad at all — and there was lots of it, which I liked, although the tea was absolutely rotten!

I asked Ivan what was in it.

"Here, Ivan, what have they put in this tea? It's stinkin'!"

"I don't quite know." He gave it a sip. "Tastes a bit like…" he sipped again. "Boy, it's weird! Ask Scaramanga; he's in the know. Hey, three tits! What's in the tea, you ugly bastard?"

Such was the repartee in that place — Oscar Wilde, eat your heart out.

"Call me 'three tits' again, McGalway, and I'll knock your fuckin' pan in, okay?!" he blurted, pointing his finger and shaking it at Ivan. "It's called Bromide!"

"Bromide, eh?" Ivan took a swig of his tea and took a long, hard swallow. "Hey, what does it do?"

I cut in at that point and told him precisely what it did. My Dad and my womb buddy, David, had warned me about what it does to the male reproductive glands. I had never experienced it before, but as a wise man once said, "A person needs new experiences, allowing them to grow. Without change, something sleeps inside us and seldom awakens. The sleeper must awaken!" *[Jay Note: the wise man in question was Duke Leto Atriedes from my favourite book and movie Dune by the mighty brain and pen of Frank Herbert and total genius that is David Lynch, respectively!]*

Ivan looked at me, then at his tea, then back to me, and then unceremoniously spat it out with an "urgh!"

Soon, breakfast was over and it was back to basic training, which I sort of enjoyed! I suppose I wanted to keep busy, to distract my mind away from admitting how depressed I actually was. Man, I wished I was home in my bed instead of in that hell of all hells, looking at all those ugly men!

We then did a little field craft, which was out in the field, funnily enough. It comprised nothing more than total boredom. I will not relate all the details. Suffice to say that the whole day was pure unadulterated tedium. I really don't remember most of what else happened that weekend. It was a blur, best left forgotten.

I was so glad to get home to Mum, Dad, Titch — and a really good cup of tea! Titch was our dog; she was a wee Jack Russell. I really loved that wee dog. She had a golden brown top coat and her belly was white. That dog could almost talk; she'd spent so much time with us!

Once, when my dad was … how shall I say? … "tipsy", he coined the never-forgotten phrase, "Happiness is dog-shaped."

"Do you know that, son?" he asked me. "Ahh, yes! Happiness is dog-shaped."

You see, when we were younger, round about the time when a child spends those damn good years of innocence, the small things around you seem large, the most significant of all being your dad and your dog. When you think they will be there, running beside you forever and ever, something happens and you realise that they won't. Dogs and people don't live forever, do they? But, sweet Jesus, I wish they could.

There were, and still are, barley fields around our house. Titch loved playing in those fields, as did my mates and my brother. When the barley grew tall and strong and ripe, we used to hide in it and call out her name. Titch always found us, bouncing up and down like a dog-torpedo, seeking us out in the long barley.

Then Titch got pregnant by some dog two doors down, another Jack Russell. I didn't witness the, erm (cough), actual act. You must remember I was about nine or ten at the time, but I managed to see them joined at the bum! A dog thing, or so I'm led to believe.

About nine weeks later, Titch gave birth to four pups, although one pup didn't make it. Snowy was her name. Fortunately, however, the other three pups survived the birth. Titch chose her spot well to give birth, right in our living room, underneath the small enclave beside the fire; that's where her tiny miracles were born. Our neighbours, the Bensons, and the whole family witnessed her births.

Her pups were born in these sack-like things; they looked like something out of the science fiction film, *Alien*. They were out of this world! Then Titch started to eat them. By the end of the third pup, the wee dog was exhausted, and so my mum helped her open the sacks, and she blew down the puppies' noses to get them breathing. By this stage, Titch was licking her puppies clean of the mucus and blood that covered them. And the smell! It was one of the most wonderful smells in the world. Nothing on Earth smells quite like newborn pups! They smell like … what do they smell like? They smell like life.

We quickly named the remaining three pups: Patch, a dog; Judy, a bitch; and finally, Jason, another dog. Jason was big, almost half the size of Titch. He was born first, then Patch, then Judy came last. If Snowy had lived, she would have been the runt of the family.

During the following weeks, Titch continued to care for her wee family. When they stopped suckling, they would seek out a feed (or a good chewing!) from the nearest finger or toe; they weren't in the least bit fussy! Their teeth were incredibly sharp! Eventually, Titch was moved into the kitchen with her pups, but Titch didn't like it in there; and so, one by one, she took each yelping pup gently in her jaws and laid them out in a line in front of the fire in the living room, where she slept, content, with her family nuzzling up to her. My Mum, bless her, reluctantly gave up, and let her stay in the living room, for a wee while, at least.

Jason was the first pup to open his eyes. It takes just a few days or so for a pup to open its eyes.

"Welcome to the world, little dog!" I said to him, scooping him up into my plastic spaceship (don't worry, it was a big plastic spaceship!) and, with a whoosh and a great deal of sound effects (supplied by yours truly) we were off, delving deep into the wide blue yonder! I gave him the grand tour of our house: upstairs and downstairs, both toilets, the kitchen, the bedrooms. Unfortunately, Jason wasn't house-trained at this point, and so you can imagine the state of my poor plastic spaceship at the end of his whimpering ordeal! Poo!

When the puppies grew up, they went to good homes. Jason went to Jerry and Sadie Haig, long-time family friends of my mum and dad. The others, Judy and Patch, went on to some of Mum's colleagues. Each of them was great fun, and we were quite sad to see those little puppies go.

Nevertheless, we still had the original one and only: our wee dog Titch. At night, we used to pile cushions on top of her and she went to sleep on the settee, snoring contented little doggy dreams! Sometimes, she would lie in front of the fire; sometimes on her belly, sometimes with all four paws up in the air. When we got up in the mornings, she was smiling — yes, dogs can smile! — and she always wagged her stubby little tail. She was house-trained but she sometimes had some accidents, and she knew when she had done something wrong.

In the years that followed, Titch became our childhood companion, our unique relationship spanning right into adolescence and puberty. Soon, Kerry, my cousin Sarah's dog, joined Titch. I should point out here that Titch once belonged to my Aunt Francis, my mother's sister.

This one day, when I was around nine years old, my Uncle Jack took his two sisters out for dinner. A meal in a restaurant was a rare occasion for my mummy (who was very wise), Aunt Francis and the rest of us. *[Jay Note: it is said that "social occasions are only warfare concealed" — a quote by Khan from Star Trek: The Original Series, episode "Space Seed."]* Anyway. My uncle had got a promotion; he was head of a famous bakery here in Northern Ireland. He taught me this rhyme:

"Barney Hughes's bread, sticks to your belly like lead,

It isn't any wonder that you fart like thunder!

After eating Barney Hughes's bread!"

[Jay Note: a quote from Barney: Bernard Hughes of Belfast, 1808-1878: Master baker, Liberal and Reformer, a book written by my dearest uncle Jack Magee]

Francis had a perfect day, her husband John doted on her. John was a security guard who worked for a security firm. They were a very close couple that spoiled themselves and their daughter Sarah equally. Sarah was a lovely wee girl with rosy cheeks and beautiful blond hair like mummy and Aunt Francis.

The following morning I heard a knock at our front door. I went downstairs to open it. I thought it was the postie — but the postman always raps the letterbox. Odd, I thought.

It was a police officer.

He was a very big man, with a flak jacket and a holstered gun.

 Oh, my God, what have I done?

David and I were young rapscallions at that age. But my mummy had a sixth sense. She was very wise. She had heard the rap too. It was Aunt Francis. My aunt had died from a brain haemorrhage.

Mummy cried and wailed at the bottom of the stairs. I had no idea what death was up until that morning. Sometimes death can be a rap on the door. Poor Uncle John lost his wife, lover and best friend — he wasn't the same man after that.

So we got possession of the dog and my cousin Sarah. Kerry was a cairn terrier and, if truth be known, she was a bit on the dim side!

Poor Kerry didn't have much of a life. A car knocked her down one night whilst Dave and I were walking the dogs. The poor thing had her pelvis crushed. Her screams still haunt me to this day. The wee dog was still alive. Fortunately, there were two young juves in the car, and they pulled over and offered to take my poor dog and me to the vet. I told David to take Titch home whilst I went on to see the vet. *[Jay Note: Juves are young juveniles, some gormless delinquents, and wasters, a bit like me at that time in my life.]*

Have you ever experienced raw, unadulterated terror, or even total blind fear? It's events like what happened that night that really shock you into reality. Everything happened so bloody fast! In the back of that car I felt it for the first time in my life — but not for the last time I should add; I felt it through this poor, crippled defenceless animal that I was holding in my arms. She was rigid with shock, and when she was moved just a little bit she started to scream in sheer agony.

The guys in the car couldn't believe this was happening to them, especially

the driver. The other guy, the passenger, looked over the passenger seat, leaned over and said to me,

"Don't worry, mate. The same thing happened to my dog, some old bastard run into him and…" He clearly realised at this point that he should shut up, thinking to himself that what he was about to say wasn't necessarily what I needed to hear! And he was right: the look I gave him could have frozen hell itself. We continued the journey in stone-cold silence.

At that stage, my dog was in deep shock: her eyes were rolled right back in their sockets, she was stiff, and her breathing was very shallow.

Why was I so calm and cool-headed? I wondered. Was I also in shock? Maybe. Even to this day, I honestly don't know.

Almost everyone in Lisburn has heard of, or at least knows of, Archbold, the vet. That's where we took the dog. It must have been half eleven at night when we finished our mercy-dash. The driver rapped fiercely on his front door, shouting,

"For God's sake, open up! We've got a dog here that's been knocked down!"

After what seemed like an eternity, Archbold opened his door. Archbold looked like a crazy, eccentric old geezer with a huge blond beard that was greying with old age. A cigarette butt hung in the corner of his mouth. He smelt of whiskey and dogs and ether. But, irrespective of how he smelt and looked, he knew his stuff; I'll give him that. We took the dog into his operating room, if you could call it that. It consisted of nothing more than an ironing board, on top of which were some old newspapers — not exactly what you'd describe as being very hygienic! He also had this big African Parrot sitting on its perch, squawking its lungs out. When it saw Kerry, it went totally berserk!

"Oh, shut up, Bob!" Archie demanded. Bob the Parrot stopped his babbling and obeyed.

"Now, let's have a look at you," he said to Kerry. Archbold put the cigarette butt behind his ear, cleared a space on the ironing board and put the dog onto it. He took Kerry by the scruff of her neck, a bit roughly I thought, and gave her an injection. I'm not quite sure what it was, but it seemed to help her. At this point, the driver cleared his throat and said to Archbold,

"Don't worry, we'll make sure the bills are paid," nodding to me. He looked at his companion, but Archbold shook his head in disagreement and said,

"No, no, no! It's quite all right, boys. Don't worry about that now." Archbold was, undoubtedly, a gentleman in every sense of the word!

He examined the poor dog. He quickly determined the problem. She had a cracked pelvis but, fortunately, none of her internal organs had been damaged. He gave her another shot; penicillin this time. She gradually came round. She pricked up her ears and looked around her. She managed a small growl at the bird and I realised Kerry was on the mend.

I was so glad to hear her voice again.

Archbold then told me I was to keep her warm in a blanket, and to give her plenty of liquids and the penicillin solution, which he provided. He then released the dog into our care.

When I got home, I thanked the boys for their help.

"We'll be in touch, of course; we want to do our bit, you understand." They then sped off into the distance, their conscience much relieved. And, true to their word, they did pay the vet his fee.

Quite soon, the wee dog was up on her feet again and everything seemed well for the next six months or so. David and I took her down the barley fields with Titch quite often, and she really enjoyed it, prancing and rolling about. A few hundred metres on from the barley fields, the farmer had some cows in a separate field. To Kerry, a city dog, they seemed like creatures from another planet. Her tiny brain couldn't comprehend such creatures! She thought David and I were big — but these things were something else entirely!

After a while, however, Kerry started to get ill and we wondered what was wrong with her. We took her back down to Archbold, who gave her a good examination. He found that her womb was full of pus and it was very serious. She had to have a hysterectomy. She had the operation and she came through it, but the wee dog, our wee puppy, was so frail that she died.

She went to the happy hunting grounds in the sky. We reasoned that it was because she had not had any pups in combination with the accident.

But we still had our other dog, Titch. She was with us for a long, long time to come.

Happy Hunting, Kerry. May you run in those barley fields forever more.

Jonathan, aged 20. Self-portrait in water-colour

CHAPTER FIVE: YOU'RE IN THE ARMY NOW!

Meanwhile, back in the future, allow me to relate to you the rest of this narrative, continuing with and concerning the story of the Weekend Warriors.

This was it: this was the big one. It was time for the twenty-day TA camp up in Camp McRats near Ballymena, in the county of Antrim. Even the name sounded ominous! *[Jay Note: Because of MOD restrictions at that time, some names of the camps and dramatis personae are disguised.]*

I said my goodbyes to Mum and Dad. My mum gave me a kiss on the cheek, and my dad shook my hand.

"Goodbye, son, and good luck — you'll enjoy it!"

Our neighbour, Gordon Davis, gave me a lift in his car down to the TA building in Lisburn. It was a fine April evening. I said goodbye to Gordon, and looked around for my mate, Ivan. I found him eventually. It was a busy scene, with everyone checking and double-checking their gear and equipment, and filling up our kit bags.

Inside, the TA hall was full of dust and blue wispy trails of cigarette smoke, which were caught in the light-beams from the late evening sun outside.

"Roll call!" the Sergeant demanded.

"*Squad!*" he shouted.

We all fell into place as we faced him.

"*Attention!*" Around thirty pairs of boots stomped firmly into place, the parade hall enduring a great echo.

"At ease, men." We assumed our position. He continued with his boring diatribe,

"As you all know, we will be leaving shortly for our training, so I want you to be absolutely sure you've got everything with you. Fall out and dismissed." He saluted and we returned the salute, turned to the right, and fell out with another click of the heels.

The TA was basically a refuge for frustrated, middle-aged men (oh, and don't forget some of those so-called professing "born again" Christians; the TA was infiltrated by one or two of them when I was there, but they always knew how to have a good time!) who wanted to get away from their wives, families, girlfriends, etc. for a weekend, where they would be free to curse, drink and shoot blanks from their guns. Enough said.

We piled up and onto the big army truck and we all trundled off into the evening. Farewell, sweet Lisburn! Missing you already! With a forlorn glance back, I reluctantly anticipated my awaiting fate.

Whilst in the truck, I tried with little success to lift our spirits with a singsong, but my comrades-in-arms were either too wrapped up in their own little thoughts or far too depressed to join in — or both. Anyway, I enjoyed myself. Here goes that immortal classic, Stan Ridgeway's Camouflage!

"I was a PFC on a search patrol huntin' Charlie down

It was in the jungle wars of '65,

My weapon jammed and I got stuck way out and all alone

And I could hear the enemy movin' in close outside

Just then I heard a twig snap and I grabbed my empty gun

And I dug in scared while I counted down my fate

And then a big marine, a giant with a pair of friendly eyes

Appeared there at my shoulder and said wait

When he came in close beside me he said,

'Don't worry, son, I'm here,

If Charlie wants to tangle now he'll have two to dodge.'

I said, 'Well thanks a lot.'

I told him my name and asked him his

And he said, 'The boys just call me Camouflage!'

Whoa, Camouflage!"

There were three more verses of this catchy little number. My comrades just ignored me; they didn't even join in with the chorus line! Pity, really; I could just imagine them doing the actions…

Quite soon, over the "event horizon", loomed the dark, brooding and imposing spires of Ballymena. By the time we arrived at our HQ, the sun was going down There was a chill wind in the air. There it was, squatting on the landscape — Camp Hell on Earth.

Welcome to Hell, I thought to myself. We then approached the gates — or should that be jaws of doom? Anyway, there was no turning back now. Our asses belonged to the Territorial Army. "My world was to become a world of shit," to use a quote from that great movie *Platoon*. As it turned out, I wasn't the only person to have watched it, and several other war films in that genre.

The gates closed behind us with a great rumble. No doubt about it, we were in the army now. We were then led through the base like sheep to the slaughter. We arrived at our "holiday chalets," which were on the third floor of a big building on the other side of the camp. This was to be our home for the next twenty days or so; we would also be out on "manoeuvres" for a night or two. We all bounded up the stairs like a herd of stampeding water-buffalo, taking the steps three at a time — well, some of us did. Inside, we found on one side of the corridor the washrooms, showers and, of course, the smelly and quite filthy obligatory latrine. On the other side were three large rooms.

The first two rooms were for our merry band of rangers. The other one was for the Corporals and the Sergeant. I must point out that there were some more rangers from other parts of the country from various battalions, who had the dubious honour of staying with us. A few of these guys were from Belfast and Enniskillen.

We were then assigned our quarters. The first group, which included Ivan, Ginge, Scaramanga, Brian, and myself, were sent into the first room. Thankfully, we were spared the maniacal and demon-like laughter of Finn, who was sent next door.

Our dormitory was on the large side. Inside, there were two rows of bunk-beds, facing each other, all of which ran along the room towards the window. It housed ten or so men on each side. That meant there were twenty horny rangers, all cooking in their own testosterone and testicles. Anyway, it also had a heavy wooden door with a large brass doorknob. The window fittings were also brass — and guess whose job it was to clean them? The floor was of bare, polished wood, and our feet echoed and reverberated deep in the floorboards when we walked on them.

Ivan and I took the bunks close to the window — a wise choice, as things turned out. We then stowed our gear in the enormous cupboards, which twinned each pair of bunks. Some smart-ass deviant with a major malfunction had scrawled graffiti in our cupboard — you know the sort of thing: phone this number for a good time; some guy's mum performs this act with barnyard animals; will fuck for food; a big phallus etc. Funny guy, har-de-fucking-har.

"Where are you two boys from?" asked a small dark, brown-eyed ranger. "The name's George, George Brown, and this here's Tommy Bean. We're both from Belfast."

We introduced ourselves.

Tommy Bean was a very tall bloke with an unusual talent, more of which we would have the pleasure of learning about a bit later on.

Looking out of our window, we could see most of the camp below us, including the parade ground. In the distance, we could also see the town of Ballymena and, beyond, the hills of Antrim. Ballymena reminded me of Lisburn and when it got dark in the evenings, the orange glow of the street lamps reminded me of home. When it got even darker, the Spring constellations began to come out: I could see Virgo and Leo, and when I stretched out I could see Arcturus, the orange red star in Bootes, the herdsman.

"Hey, Fisher, close that fuckin' window!" an ignorant ranger called out.

I tutted and, with a heavy sigh, I obliged the waiting ranger.

Very soon after, it was time for lights out. All we needed now was some wise guy to play the mouth-organ in the darkness. But no one could, and that was the end of that. *[Jay Note: I should point out to you, dear reader, that I am not referring to a sexual act or any kind of homoerotic behaviour or ambiguity; no, I am simply referring to a harmonica.]*

The night passed very slowly, and I hardly slept. My heart was pounding. My second favourite organ — my brain (thanks, Woody) — was full of adrenaline, half afraid of what would happen to us come morning. I tried to keep one eye open, but I eventually succumbed to the gnawing tiredness.

[Jay Note: this quotation is attributed to Woody Allen's character in his only sci-fi movie: Sleeper.]

Without any warning, the door exploded — or it seemed that way. Three men burst into the room. They were like a trio of mad dervishes, whirling like, well, dervishes, I suppose.

The first man, a small, fat, ginger-moustached lance-corporal kicked at the first bed, waking a stunned ranger. Before he could say "What the fu—?!" his cupboard and all his gear crashed onto the floor with a huge bang; this was the handiwork of another corporal — a tall, thin man. They looked a little like Laurel and Hardy. The last was the Sergeant — Sergeant Major Cowenson. By this stage, we leapt down from our beds, totally and automatically scared rigid to attention, by our bunks, standing in our bare feet.

"Okay, Ladies." His voice grated through his moustache across the room. His voice of command was deep, rough, authoritative, and grated like sandpaper. The Sarge was a little on the small side, but he was built like a brick outhouse. This guy was hard; so hard, I reckoned, that he pissed gravel and shit concrete bricks — he was that hard!

He continued. *"I am your drill sergeant, Major Cowenson. If I get any shit out of you pussies, I will rip your heads off and shit down your necks!"*

Oooh! Who's been watching *Heartbreak Ridge*? I thought silently to myself.

George Brown then whispered in my ear.

"Man, we are reamed, big time!"

The Sarge overheard this, and marched over towards us and shouted,

"Okay, fuck for brains, which one of you wise fuckers said that? *No talking in the ranks!*"

"It was me Sergeant," I lied. (Just call me Spartacus.) I thought fast and I replied even faster, "I said, err, um, I wish I was… dreaming all this. Sorry, Sir."

"Don't call me *Sir*," he roared back at me, a fleck of spittle from his mouth hitting me in the face. I winced back.

"I work for a living! And don't be sorry, be right! Now hit the deck and give me twenty!"

Push-ups were the Armed Forces' universal basic form of punishment, I suppose.

"Ahh, fuck it! You're *all* doin' twenty!" Cowenson added with a sadistic gleam in eye. I do reckon the Sarge enjoyed watching all these young men prostrating themselves before him in a perverse way and manner. His moustache was very YMCA…

When the moaning, groaning and heaving ceased, we were then shown how to make our bed-blocks, thanks to Corporals McPoguemahole and O'Farquar.

"Now, hear this," Cowenson bellowed to us all. "Get your boots on, it's time for a run!"

We endured a run through the camp. I took a quick glance at my watch. It read zero five-thirty hours. Half five in the fraggin' morning.

Afterwards, we had a wash-up in the bathrooms. The day's timetable went like this:

Zero six hundred hours: Wash up, empty the bladder, or to use the vernacular, take one's piss and empty one's bowels — or take a shit, to use the Anglo-Saxon.

Zero six-thirty hours: head back to the barracks to clean up and put on our uniforms and "bull" our boots — that was slang for polishing them. We all had two pairs of boots: one for parade, the other for the field or the (gulp!) battleground!

Zero seven hundred hours until zero eight hundred hours:

breakfast in the mess hall. It was spick and span, clean as a whistle. The hall was bright and decorated with military regalia. As it came to our turn, Ivan cursed bitterly.

"Oh, no! Not more fuckin' bromide!"

Zero eight hundred hours: time for parade. This event occurred every day at the same time for the following two weeks. If you missed it, you'd be put on report, which would ultimately translate to more push-ups and a lot of more verbal abuse. To quote the Sergeant: "I will rip your heads off and shit down your necks!" Alternatively, there was my favourite anecdote: "I will personally rip your eye balls out and skull-fuck you!" Yet another use of the English Language to make Oscar Wilde turn in his grave. Anyway, this malarkey went on and on for as long as the Sergeant wanted it to. We marched. We were drilled, in the military sense, mind you, and not in the dentistry sense, but equally just as painful.

Twelve hundred hours: chow time. That was a welcome relief; we could rest our weary limbs. Then on to the lecture hall, which was where we all learnt basic first aid. That's when I was introduced to the weekend warriors' handbook, "Survive to Fight." It was full of scary diagrams and all that shit that goes down during a nuclear apocalypse. What the book did not tell us, in the case that Armageddon was unleashed onto this beautiful world, is what any sane person would do. I would get on my knees, turn around and kiss my sweet ass goodbye.

Thirteen hundred hours: onto the firing range. We had to wear our armour, that is, our helmets. When the Quartermaster saw the size of my head as we were being fitted with our webbing he remarked,

"Fuck me, Fisher, you've got a big head!" He then issued me with an extra large one. Whey hey! Extra large one — get it? Sounds a bit rude, doesn't it? Never mind. Anyway, back onto the firing range, that was situated inside one of the large buildings that dotted the barracks. We were given a weapon, an SLR (self-loading rifle). We were not allowed to refer to it as a gun, nor were we allowed to handle the new (at that time) SA80. That was a shame, because it sure looked class — much more… groovy! *[Jay Note: the word "Groovy" was a favourite quote for all of us at the comic* shop. *We said "Groovy" every time we watched the cult classic movie Evil Dead II, with the mighty and legendary actor Bruce Campbell who played Ash. More memorial one-liners from this absolutely classic film we used to quote were, "Chainsaw!"; "Necronomicon Ex Mortis"; "Let's carve ourselves a witch"; and of course, my favourite, "Yo! She-bitch, let's go!"]* Unfortunately, however, we had to use small shells on the indoor range for safety's sake. We put our ear defenders on. We were told when to fire from the belly position. It's not like you see in the movies; for one example, take John Rambo (Sly Stallone) in *First Blood*. Okay, you don't charge the enemy from the belly position — that's the most accurate firing position — and you usually don't scream from the top of your lungs, 'Die! Die, you mother fuckers!' like the Marines out of the sci-fi movie *Aliens*; no, sir, you would give away your position; no, sir, that's not the TA-way! We just crawl on our bellies! Those who crawl on their bellies live to fight another day! That should be the Territorial motto, in my humble opinion. Oh, and another note: we certainly don't wear bandannas around our foreheads!

Fifteen hundred hours: NCB (Nuclear, Chemical, Bacterial) drill, which was bloody fraggin' scary. This involved donning our NCB gear — ie gloves, masks, boots, and the whole enchilada.

"Okay, shit-heads," Corporal Clunk began (he was the guy in charge of the gas chamber and was a right clunk).

"When I say so, I want you all to take off your masks then shout *"Gas! Gas!"* into your masks. You will experience a bitter smell and a stinging sensation in your eyes. This is CS gas, as used in the case of crowd control. It's also known as Tear Gas."

We all held our breaths in unison as the tank began to fill with the gas. Why am I here? I asked myself. I could be home with Mum and Dad and the dogs. Am I out of my fraggin' mind? For the first time — and not for the last time, I might add — I was really homesick, complete with real home pangs. Mad Jock Mac Fock was one of the other corporals involved in this exercise (don't ask me how he got his nickname, I just made it up).

"Now!" he barked in his Scottish accent. As one man we shouted,

"*Gas! Gas! Gas!*" into the breathing apparatus and donned our masks.

"*Do not*, I repeat, *do not* scratch your eyes!" The guy was a comedian. I mean, how could we? We were wearing rubber gloves for frag's sakes! We were then forced to run around the compound. It was very heavy going and then some. But, I must admit, I really dug the machismo of it all. And, hey, it's not every day a guy can dress up in a rubber suit!

Seventeen hundred hours: time for supper. First, we would get out of our togs and then we spent a well-deserved hour feeding our faces with everything we could get our paws on and in our faces. It was a feeding frenzy!

Eighteen hundred hours: back on the parade ground for yet another hour of parading and stomping of our feet. It was typical, early April weather: a mix of sunshine and showers. A fine mist was drizzling from the Antrim hills. Through the red haze, the sun was going down. Our boots shone almost blood-red in the dampness.

The left hand of Jonathan, by Jonathan

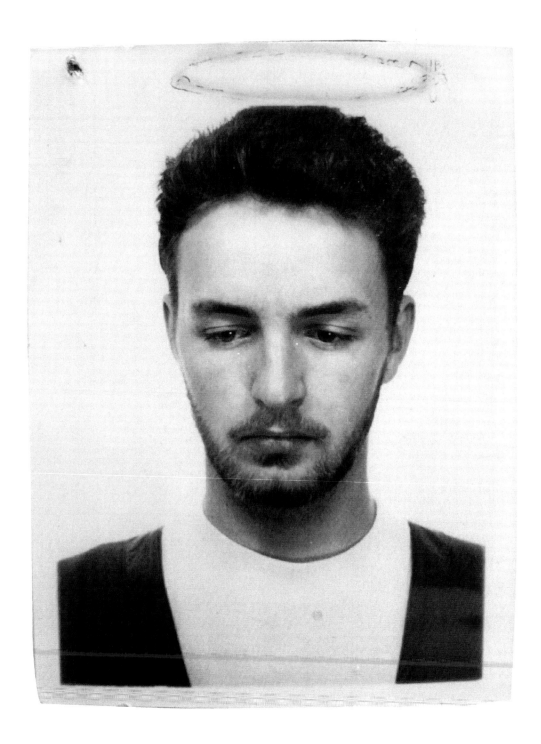

Jonathan with halo

CHAPTER SIX: THE NUMBER OF THE BEAST

By twenty hundred hours we were dismissed and I, for one, was so glad; I was totally exhausted. Is this how David, my womb buddy, had felt when he was doing his training? I made a mental note to ask Mum and Dad. Oh, how I missed them! The home pangs were back with a vengeance. When time permitted (after the chores in the barracks), I went with Ivan to the NAAFI, to do an ET — Phone Home. *[Jay Note: ET, the Extra-Testicle (sorry, dear reader, for that joke; that should be Extra-Terrestrial), was a soppy and sad little movie concerning a sad and soppy diminutive alien by the same name directed by Steven Spielberg. Just what on Earth was he thinking?]*

"Hello, Mum?" I said in a quivering, high-pitched squeaking voice.

"Err, it's me. Are things, you know, are things okay?"

I tried to eradicate the emotion out of my voice — and failed completely. I was feeling miserable, really miserable. I poured my heart out to my mum and dad in that, cold, freezing phone box.

"Listen, Mum, I — I don't know if I can hack this... It's not the training — I can do that — but," I stuttered, "it's the way we're being treated. They're like a bunch of wild savages in this place!"

I was careful with my choice of words: it was my mother I was talking to, and she doesn't like bad language; she brought us up to know better.

As she is so fond of saying, "Cursing and swearing — it's not big and it's not clever."

"Jonathan, love, I know it feels bad, but give it a day or two and see how you feel; you know that we've no transport…" she said earnestly. "Wait, I'll put your Father on… Billy!" she shouted after my dad, "It's Jonathan!"

After a brief pause, my Father came on the line. I heard him whisper,

"Who?" and then he said, "Oh!" (I think my Mum kicked him or nudged him into waking up!) "Hello, son, how are you keeping?"

"Gee, swell, I'm having a whale of a time, a whale of a time! Cheers, Dad! Thanks for those awe-inspiring words of encouragement!"

"Now, don't get sarcastic with me, your old man, son!"

"Sorry, Dad, but—"

"But nothing! You don't want to be a failure in front of your mates, do you? That's the worst thing you could ever do!"

"I guess you're right, Dad." I sighed a heavy sigh. "There's the pips. How's Titch?"

"She's fine, son, just fine."

"I hope you're feeding her well?"

"We are, son, we are."

"I'll ring tomorrow. Say goodbye to Mum for me. See you both soon."

Still depressed, Ivan and myself went into the NAAFI building. Yep, you guessed it: another bar, but at least it had a TV room; that was, at least, a bonus. Inside the bar, there was a jukebox — another bonus; it was, however, being monopolised by Ginge and Brown, the "Portadown Brigade." They were very fond of that song by the Bangles, "Eternal Flame." It was, in fact, being "eternally" played on that jukebox. I think it reminded them of their girlfriends; "our song" sort of thing. They looked seriously depressed, sitting at one of the tables that was close to that infernal jukebox, complete with beers in their hands.

"Hold my hand, darling, do you feel my heart beating?

Do you understand? Do you feel the same? Am I only dreaming?

Is this feeling an eternal flame?

Close my eyes, sunshine through the rain,

A whole life without you, come and feel my pain.

I don't want to lose this feeling, ohh…

Is this burning an eternal flame?"

Yada, yada, yada, and so on and so forth. I left them to their alcoholic-induced pleasures and went to the barracks, up the stairs to the dormitory, where I did a little ironing to keep busy as much as I could. I was feeling lonely, horny and just a little pissed off; I craved excitement. Then I whispered to Ivan,

"To hell with this, come with me. I'm gonna do my party piece."

He returned my whisper and said, "Are you sure?"

"You'd better believe it!" I whispered back.

We both went into the bathroom, and I told Ivan to keep an eye out.

"Colgate, eh? I'll give 'em Colgate!" I then proceeded to use my toothpaste to make my mouth full of foam, water and saliva. Then I nodded to Ivan, and we both went back inside the dorm.

All the rangers were there, including Ginge and Brian, all of whom had returned from their session in the bar. All was quiet when we sat down. I started to bull my boots; things seemed normal. I winked at Ivan, he sniggered and looked away. That was the signal.

I stood up, clutched at my bedpost, then at George with my other hand.

"Hey, Fisher, what's wrong?"

All eyes were on me as I collapsed, moaning and writhing, wide-eyed staring down onto the floor. I started flailing my arms and legs about, thrashing around — and then I began foaming at the mouth.

"Sufferin' fuck!" George exclaimed, immediately coming to my aid. "Fisher's havin' an epileptic fuckin' fit!"

"Holy shit!" Brian added. "Someone get the fuckin' Corporal! Get his mouth open! Get his mouth open! Don't let him swallow his fuckin' tongue!"

I am forced to admit this — for a weekend warrior, Brian knew his stuff. He must have done a first aid course or something. Or maybe he just picked it up from the television. Yeah. Probably the latter.

"That won't be necessary, thanks all the same to you all," I said, quite calmly and succinctly. I stood up. "It's only toothpaste! Haven't you guys seen that John Carpenter film, *The Thing*? You should have seen your faces! God, I wish I had a camera! That was a total classic!" Then, with a great deal of nonchalance, I wiped the slobbers off with my trusty towel. As a great writer once wrote, "A man's not a man unless he knows where his towel is." *[Jay Note: the great writer in question is the late, great Douglas Adams; what a guy, RIP.]*

Ivan creased up with laughter. George looked at me with new-found respect. Ginge looked at me with disgust, but Brian laughed and shook his head, then said, "You are alright, Fisher; weird, but alright."

Scaramanga added, "You are one weird bastard, Fish Cake, one weird bastard!"

"Well, so are you, you ugly bastard, and don't you dare call me a "bastard" again."

I grabbed his skinny, slimy neck.

"My name's Jonathan Fisher, not 'Fish Cake'. You hear me?"

I shook his neck. "And I know who my father is, okay?"

I let go of his greasy neck and said,

"Good. I'm glad that's settled. Don't get me angry. You wouldn't like me when I'm angry." Cue the *Incredible Hulk* theme tune!

Later on that evening, when things were quietening down for the night, we discovered Tommy Bean's talent: he could play "God Save The Queen" and "The Sash" quite distinctly on his bottom — by breaking wind!

That was a typical day in the life of a reluctant weekend warrior. Lights out, twenty three hundred hours.

"Parp parb parpy parpy paaaaarppp parp parb parbbbbbbb. Parp."

The whole dormitory exploded in a fit of laughter.

"Suffering fuck," I thought and I fell into a light slumber.

Jonathan, aged 20. Self-portrait in water colour

Chapter Seven: 7-7-7 Is My Name

For the next three weeks, we lived — more or less — by the same old humdrum routine, apart from the time when we went up north to Camp O'Helligan.

My comrades and I were marching double-quick time across a beach. It was a warm morning and the sun was shining down on our heads. My comrade, George Brown, was singing, "When, will I, will I be famous?"

I joined in with the chorus, "I can't answer that! When will we see our pictures in the papers?" *[Jay Note: these song lyrics are by Bros., a cheesy pop trio beloved by teenyboppers.]* We were pounding our feet to the rhythm of the music in our heads, in our chests. There was a hint of salt in the air. We were leaving our footprints behind in the wet sand.

Later on that day, we were inspected in the field by some snooty bigwig officer, a major or something like that. The guy was English. We were busy taking a break. I was so tired; I wanted a rest. I lay down in the grass with my hands behind my head, using my headgear as a pillow, nonchalantly chewing on a blade of grass. He was giving the troops the sort of small talk you see Prince Charles and the Queen giving at garden parties. He passed George, Ivan and Brian (who almost collapsed during the twenty km march). They all stood up for this guy, but I didn't. I bow to no man. Then he walked in front of the sun.

I shaded my eyes and looked up at him, and thought to myself, yeah? Do you want something, bub? What's to ya? You're spoiling my suntan!

"What's your name, ranger?" he asked in a posh voice.

"Fisher, Sir," I replied with my best Belfast accent.

"Where are you from, Ranger Fisher?"

"Lisburn, Sir."

There was an awkward silence. He fidgeted his feet, coughed and said,

"Jolly good. Well, carry on."

When he went out of my line of sight, Ivan sat down beside me and said,

"Are you mad, Johnny? He could have had your balls for that!"

"I doubt it, Ivan. I would have stood up and addressed the officer if Cowenson was there, but he wasn't. Cowenson was at the other edge of the field having a smoke with his Corporals."

During the night, we had to guard a forest from attack. Why? Don't ask me why — our job was but to do or die; "into the valley of death rode the six hundred", and so on. It was a coniferous forest and it was thick with pine trees, so much so that I couldn't see the forest for the trees and I couldn't see any stars. It was that thick and dense. It's true what they say about forests: they're very, very quiet and they smell great.

As a wise guy once stated, "If a tree falls in the forest and no one is there to hear it, does it make a sound?" Yeah. Very Zen.

All I could see in the darkness were the dim lights of cigarettes, all glowing red and pale red, dimmer shades and then brightening red again. The red lights moved around the black, slowly, back and forth, and back and forth. Behind each light there was a man; a man with thoughts of home and hearth, duty, his fears, loved ones — and, of course, the prime mover, sex.

There was no light before me — but I definitely had sex on the brain and in my loins too. Man, but did I!

Slowly, very slowly, the dawn came. I tried to have a doze during the night, but it's hard to get a little shut-eye whilst wearing full combat gear and webbing. To solve the problem, we took turns at watch duty and, when the morning came, I relieved myself up the nearest tree. Ahh, sweet relief!

Time for field rations. They were simply beautiful; it was just like camping out.

It was there, deep in that forest glen, that I devised my Mega-Plan, the ultimate, secret defence weapon for the future…I was going to need it

Soon, it was back to Camp O'Helligan for a good hearty breakfast, and then onto the firing range for a bit of target practice. It was open-air in a field close to the border of Donegal. The surrounding countryside was breathtaking and nothing short of picturesque: that's MOD property for you; unspoilt and undisturbed — apart from the Army Yahoos and the TA weekend warriors, that is!

It was a warm, spring day. The field itself was on some marshland, and it was there, on that field, that I spotted a small newt for the first time in my life. The little creature was just sitting there, basking in the sunlight, enjoying life's simplest but most amazing treasures.

This primordial beast transfixed me. This little thing was indeed rare, and probably close to extinction. All the surrounding countryside was undoubtedly the newt's natural habitat. I wasn't the only person that was interested in my little newt friend: Corporal McPoguemahole came over and looked at what I was looking at. And it was then, when he saw the newt that he stomped on it with his army issue boot.

"God, damn it!" I said furiously. "What did you go and do that for?"

The Corporal ignored me.

I have the notion that the newt survived the vicious attack; they are quick wee things, and the species has been on this mud-ball of a planet far longer than the ape-men, such as Pougemahole, the big monkey-slapper

Shortly after, we had to start shooting our weapons. We were issued live rounds. Ear defenders on, load, lock and check.

Corporal Mac Fock was lying beside me as I started shooting.

"Okay, son, put your shoulder into it; breathe deep and fire your weapon as you exhale. Line your sight up to the target, gently squeeze the trigger and *fire!*"

Blammmmmmm! My ears almost exploded as the bullet ripped through the air and almost instantaneously hit the target about seven, eight or even nine hundred metres away. Or was it almost a thousand? Who can say? The recoil of the SLR hit my shoulder, numbing it hard. It was the loudest noise *I have ever heard in my entire life* — even with my EDs in!

Blammmmmmm! Blammmmmmm! Blammmmmmm! I let off three more rounds, all equally as painful. I shut my eyes as I winced from the pain.

I don't know how to describe that feeling but, well, it felt kind of wrong — well, all wrong. It was my conscience, and my sense of self-right and ethics telling me to stop, but I just continued: orders are orders, after all, and so I continued firing.

Have you ever seen those old pictures of that "experiment" on the television wherein a man is put into a room and told to administer electric shocks of various intensities to a "learner" in a booth? When the learner in the booth screams out, begging him to stop, the other guy, "a teacher", just simply continues — and for no other reason than because he was ordered to do so by an authority figure; without blinking, he continues on with the torture — until, that is, the learner in the booth passes out from the pain.

"Please continue the agony!"

"The experiment insists you must continue!"

"You have no choice in this matter!"

There are always choices.

[Jay Note: the infamous experiment was called The Milgram experiment on obedience to authority figures. I despised all authority figures — and then some.]

But that was just television. This was real life — and it was happening to me.

This ethical dilemma was not hard for me to resolve: I could not fire this weapon at another human being. That was essentially the bottom line.

Recognising that thought, I started to wonder about the making and manufacturing of these terrible, lethal weapons; it was disgusting and horrible.

It was time for a judgement call and so, there and then, I decided when this exercise was over I would leave this fools' army. At that point, it was only a couple of more days until the end— I could hack it until then.

The passing out parade; man, that was a joke and a half. I was now a fully trained, motherfucking-mad-for-it killing machine. I could strip, clean and reassemble an SLR, a hand-held sub-machine-gun, and a heavy-machine-gun. I was impervious to attack by nuclear, biological and chemical attack from the evil ministrations and the forces of the Soviet Empire. I was a weekend warrior; I was a soldier. So, why didn't I feel like one? I certainly looked the part. Was I a conscientious objector?

"My Mudda and my Fadda" came to see me at Camp "Grenada" Ballymena for the passing out parade. It reminded me of the song of the same name and the situation I was in. Anyway, I did feel a certain mount of jingoistic pride as we marched in unison, and I felt a tingle up my spine. Afterwards, we had a group photograph, copies of which were far too expensive, and so I asked my Mudda to take a photo of me parading around. We all met up in the bar: Gordon Davis, our next-door neighbour from two doors down and a long-time family friend, had brought my parents up to Ballymena as we hadn't a car at the time. I greeted my mum and dad in the usual fashion and shook Gordon's hand, thanking him for looking after my parents.

Let's talk about cars for a moment and, in particular, the cars that my father owned during his lifetime. He loved his cars. I can remember one night; I must have been, let's see now, nine or ten at the time. My dad got his car stolen by some evil bastard or bastards, from right in front of our door. The car was reported missing. A few days later, the police found it burnt-out in Twinbrook, a notorious part of Belfast. The number-plate of the car was the only surviving relic. To make matters worse, the insurance company, that my dad had paid into, totally reamed him, refusing to cough up the cash at the time. Bloody vultures and bloody bastards. I don't know who were worse: the insurance people or the thieving scum who did that to our family. Hold that thought for a moment: is there a difference?

You know, I can still see my Father standing in front of the fireplace (one of his favourite spots), smoking a cigarette but hardly taking a drag, letting the smoke stain the ceiling. He was like a caged, trapped animal — feuding with the insurance company, muttering and brooding under his breath.

The situation was bad. Only a few months earlier he had lost his job, where he had worked as a manager in Olympia Typewriters. He was never quite the same man after that: it diminished him. After the aforementioned bastards stole his car, his blood pressure rocketed and hit the roof. And, as per the old saying, bad luck comes in threes: the third strike was the passing of Granddad Fisher, who died only a little time after the first two blows. It was a terrible time, though undoubtedly worse for Granny Fisher, who subsequently hit the bottle big time. That's why I don't drink alcohol: it turned my sweet old granny into a sweet old alcoholic.

Anyway, back to cars. The most totally utterly and embarrassing event to have happened to me at that time was when David and I were coming home by ferry from Liverpool. We had been in Stratford-upon-Avon on a school trip to see Shakespeare's Macbeth. We were in fourth year, aged fifteen. I was seasick there and back; David wasn't. Well, he did join the Royal Navy when he was seventeen.

The car in question was a small hatchback. Picture the scene, if you can: we are at the Belfast Dockyard, and all my fellow school chums are leaving the boatyard in their big, swanky posh cars, the bastards. My dad has this small hatchback; it is second-hand with a few million miles on the clock (I am exaggerating, of course). My father asks us to put our rucksacks into the back of the car: David put in his first, and then it is my turn, only it won't fit, and so I force it in and close the boot. There was an almighty bang and, as luck would have it (or sheer stupidity), the rear window of the car simply shattered into smithereens! There were millions of tiny glass cubes everywhere! Man, I could not talk; my jaw just dropped wide open, hitting the deck beneath me! What have I done? Why, oh why does all the weird shit happen to me?

My dad just said very softly and quietly,

"Jonathan, get in the car." When my dad's quiet like that, that's code for shit, man, he's raging. I obeyed instantly, without question.

No one spoke on the way home to Lisburn, partly because no one would dare speak and partly because the wind was howling all around us, through the broken window. With hindsight, it seems almost comical and funny, hilarious even, but not then. My dad was livid, and I felt so low and depressed, not to mention totally scundered.

When we got home, I said to my dad,

"Don't worry, I'll clean it up."

My dad simply replied, "Yes, you will."

And I did — eventually.

The next day, my dad went to the scrap yard to see if he could find a replacement for the rear window, and he did — eventually.

The next most shameful moment of my life occurred a few years later, and that, too, involved a motorcar — or, to be more precise, a police car.

It happened one Thursday afternoon. Marty Møller and I were on our way home from the comic shop. I had left my push-bike at the Danish Palace (the Møller family residence; their "stately home," if you will). Anyway, gentle reader, we were on the way home through the winding avenues and roundabouts of Lisburn, with its treacherous byways and highways, when I was brutally, quite without mercy or warning, savagely set upon by a cop car!

Right, this is the situation — this is how it happened.

Marty walked over to the traffic island, and on to safety. Then he walked to the Candy Box, a newsagent's, and he shouted over,

"Come on, Johnny, what's the hold-up?"

"Coming, now," I shouted back in reply.

Still thinking of comics, sex, rock'n' roll and world domination (but not necessarily in that order, mind you) — and, maybe, just maybe, I was daydreaming a little (I had a lot of things on my mind in those teenage days), I stepped into the moving traffic — and then bounced off a car! Like Starsky and Hutch and TJ Hooker (although back then I had more hair than Shatner) I rolled over in slow motion! But I was okay; I had reached the sanctuary of the traffic island. And it was then that I saw out of the corner of my eye the car pulling over.

Holy shit! I thought to myself as I saw what was coming out of the car!

It was the filth, the pigs, the fuzz, the peelers, the cops. It was the Royal Ulster Constabulary!

"Err, sorry about that, Officers," I said most apologetically, my heart pounding and my throat drying up as I spoke. Fear and adrenaline — don't ya just love them?

Officer D, who was driving the car, said quite angrily,

"You know, son, that was a dangerous stunt you tried to pull off there!"

Officer C, Officer's D's partner, chipped in,

"You know jaywalking is a serious offence!"

Is it hell! I thought to myself.

"Name and address, please," Officer D asked.

I had to oblige; they had guns! But they didn't take down my details. They asked me what I was doing, where I was going, etc. Meanwhile, Marty, the wee git, had ducked behind a parked car. Looking out from his vantage point he was laughing his nuts off, while my brain and senses were locked in almost mortal combat, trying to worm myself out of the dire predicament!

"Listen, Officers, I was just on my way home with my friend here."

But Marty had done his disappearing act (he hid himself round the corner again, but I knew he was there; I could sense and smell the dirty rat!).

"I know that it was a stupid and dumb thing to do," I put my head on my shoulders, twisted my foot in the dirty tarmac, and tried to look as innocent as possible — the kind of look that Jake Elwood — John Belushi, you know the guy who overdosed (or was it his brother?) in *The Blues Brothers* movie — gave to Carrie Fisher, she of Princess Leia fame, towards the end. That was the sort of look I gave the two RUC constables. Yes, they were a pair of right constables!

They stood a while longer and gave me a lecture on road safety and all that other crap. All the time, I was nodding in agreement, thinking,

Yes, Officer. No, Officer. Absolutely, Officer. Whatever you say, Officer. Three bags full, Officer.

Eventually, they let me go — with a warning. I quickly hurried away, rushing around the corner of the Candy Box newsagents where Marty Møller was lurking in wait for me.

"Oh, Johnny, that was the funniest thing I've seen in my entire life!" He was doubled up with laughter and could hardly stand. "You ever seen *Top Cat*? You were TC and those cops were Officer Dibble!

'Good evening, Officer Dibble! How are you today, Officer Dibble?'"

Then he started singing the theme tune —

"Top Cat! The indisputable Top Cat!

His close friends call him TC,

Providing they pay a fee!

Top Cat! The indisputable leader of the gang!

He's the Top, he's the championship,

He's the tip-top cat — Top Cat!"

"I'm so glad you found it so fraggin' funny, Martin!" I said, pushing him away.

"Why didn't you help me out back there, you jerk?" I was so mad at him.

"I can't believe you did that. Yeah, go and catch some real criminals, you — you — constables!" I shouted back at the police car. I gave them the time-honoured one-finger salute.

"Go spin on this!"

To this day, Marty Møller has never let me forget that incident. Looking back at it now, I think it's fraggin' hilarious!

Where was I? Oh, yes, we were still at my passing out parade. The parade finished with all the usual pomp and ceremony. We all ended back at the NAAFI for some drinks, where we met the other rangers' families. It was soon time for my parents and all the others to go home. I told them to expect me home later, and to get a good cup of tea and a warming feed ready.

Most of us went upstairs to our rooms to wait for the appropriate trucks to arrive to take us back to where we belonged — to our own individual TA bases. Soon after, we were allowed to wear our civilian clothes. Ivan and I got our rucksacks out of the graffiti cupboard, and shut it for the last time ever.

"Guess we'll never know where to go for a 'good time' eh, Johnny?" Ivan said, referring to the phone number in our cupboard.

"Yeah, right," I said.

It was a late Sunday afternoon in May. The windows were open to let the warm spring air in; the bright sunlight moved across the room, ever so slowly.

No one spoke as we waited to leave. I was wondering what poor sucker would be in these bunks tomorrow, or even later on tonight, when the next cadre came bounding up those steps.

The truck came for us around eighteen hundred hours. I said my goodbyes to George Brown and Tommy Bean.

"See you guys around. Jesus, has it been twenty days? It feels like a lifetime!" I shook their hands.

"Sure thing! We'll probably see you around Belfast. We'll go for a drink!" Brown said.

Sure, Brown, I thought to myself, and swine will fly under an azure moon.

Why do people always, always say that sort of bullshit when they don't, or won't, ever mean it? True to form, you never see them ever again. Pity, really; I kinda liked those two Joes. And yes, I never did see them again.

By the time we were back at HQ in Lisburn, it must have been around twenty hundred hours. It was time for debriefing and then home, sweet home.

I said goodnight to Ivan, Finn and Brian; they weren't a bad bunch, I suppose. We were a team and, thanks to them all, I was never healthier, or more fit and agile. Thanks to all of you in The Territorial Army and her Majesty's Royal Irish Rangers for giving me the experience of a lifetime. Wherever you may be, comrades in arms, I salute you all (even if I do still think you were all a bunch of monkey-slappers!).

I walked home from the TA centre with a spring in my step, a zing in my ying, and a song on my lips, whistling home with my rucksack on my shoulder. I was a happy man. Correction: I was a *free* man. *Yessssss!* I punched the air with my fist.

For the very first time in my life, I had money. I would put a little in the bank, and give half to my mum.

When I arrived home, my dog Titch (or Chien — that's French for dog, as we used to affectionately call her) was all over me with excitement.

"Yeah, yeah. Later for you, dog," I said to her — I had another woman upstairs, waiting my arrival, in my room, under my bed. She lived in a magazine called *"Playboy!"*

Ohhh yesssss! Ohhh, babyyy! Ohhh, yesssss! Oh sweet mystery of life, at last I've found you!

Well, it was twenty days without it, after all!

My Neighbour Karolyn, by Jonathan

Jonathan, aged 21. Self-portrait on coloured paper

CHAPTER EIGHT: BORN FREE

So, after precisely one week of freedom, I decided to hand my kitbag back to the TA. One of the born-again Christian soldiers, Sergeant McGodsquad, asked me if I was doing the right thing.

"Are you sure you're doing the right thing, my son?" He clutched my shoulder, hard, and looked at me like I was a sinner to be saved.

I was born once and christened once — and that's enough for me and my faith. Now that's just my own opinion, and it's my right as an individual to say that, so, get off my back, God boy! I thought to myself. I didn't say that to his face, despite being sorely tempted. No, I just told him I wanted to join the navy (I lied).

"The Navy, you say? The Navy, you say? A fine institution, my boy, a fine institution, indeed. But aren't they full of gays and homosexuals?"

"My twin brother is in the senior service," I said to him, "and he is definitely not gay!"

He relaxed his arm from my shoulder and quickly took it away. He kicked my kitbag right across the hall. He then issued me with my discharge papers, which I quickly signed. I saluted Sergeant McGodsquad and thanked him.

On the way home, my heart was heavy. What have I done? Had I passed over the "crossroads" of my life? Had I made a fatal error? Did I have to lie to them? My thoughts were dark and I was feeling very depressed as I walked through Laurelhill High School's tennis courts (I could still make out my **"CH☺PPER LIVES!"** graffiti scrawl on the wall!). I hung my head low, kicking the gravel as I went along. Then, as I walked round the corner, I heard a sweet, female, angelic voice, and it said,

"Oh, hi, Jay!"

Oh, sweet mystery of life, at last I've found you! It was Janet Black, my oldest friend Rick Black's sister. She was playing tennis with one of her school chums. She was a total flirt, but I was strangely hypnotised by the way she had grown up and matured; that, her sweating body and the way she just glowed. Oh, and the way she moved and smelled! She was a woman — and, as it turned out, my first real crush.

"Oh, hi, err, there, Janet." I fumbled for words to say; she'd taken me by surprise.

"I'm sorry, Janet, I've got a lot on my mind. Must go. Sorry." That's all I could say at that moment and, obviously, I was totally mortified. Oh, very good, Jonathan. Superb repertoire, I must say, I thought to myself. Clap, clap, clap.

At that moment, all I could think about was Janet; she changed my life, albeit very subtly. I think she turned my way of thinking around, and she certainly rid me of thinking about the TA. I think my thought process went something like, What TA? These were strange feelings I was experiencing; very confusing.

Well, what now? I asked myself. I've burned that bridge behind me.

But, as my old mentor-to-be, lifetime friend and fellow Astrozombie, Richard Munn, would say:

"There is always a solution! It's just knowing how to find it, that's the problem!"

Richard the Munnisher

The Munnisher

CHAPTER NINE: THE MUNNISHER COMETH

Richard Munn. These are the only words I can use to describe this guy: big hairstyle, good chess player, superb guitar player, big *Punisher* fan, damn good friend.

I first met Rick Munn, or the Munnisher as he came to be known, in the comic shop. He had a liking for that totally inferior to Judge Dredd comic book, *The Punisher*. I met him the Saturday after leaving the TA.

The Munnisher went to Wallace High School, like Marty. He had a curly mane of long brown hair with brown inquisitive eyes, and a formidable stocky build. For his size, he was … what's the word? … diminutive, but he was like a miniature Hercules. He was a real powerhouse of a guy. Well, anyway, that's quite enough flattery for now. On with the story.

"What's that thing you're holding?" I asked him.

He was demonstrating his *Marvel* comics' "Crime Viewer." He held it up to the window to let the sunlight in though the viewer. It was like a pair of binoculars, only they're not crap. It showed various *Marvel* comics' superheroes in glorious 3D action (trade mark). It was a crude slide-player, a tacky kaleidoscope — although kaleidoscopes are infinitely more entertaining, at least in my book of "Entertaining and Cosmic Facts", that is.

"Wow, that's, like, totally awesome, man," I yawned in boredom.

He looked up at me from his superhero-induced fantasies and said,

"Well, who is your comic book hero then, Fisher? *The Punisher?*"

I scoffed at this remark, and chuckled very hard at him for saying such a foolish thing. The poor misguided child had known nothing else in his comic book life apart from *DC Comics* and the comic-filth *Marvel*, both of which were produced from their respective bowels.

"No, no, no!" I shook my head in utter disgust. "Get thee behind me, Satan!"

Paul Andrews looked up from where he was sitting on the floor at the back of the shop, cross-legged and reading a dubious comic book called *Sandman* (for sad bastards or "Goths-R-Us-Monthly", as it was more commonly known).

"No, I'm not referring to you, Andrews, go on back to your pit!"

"Anyway, Dick, as I was saying," I looked back at Paul Andrews, just to make sure that he was still visible to the naked eye, and then turned my attention back to Rick Munn and said,

"My favourite comic hero of all time is Judge Dredd — respect the badge!"

Then, out of the void of the space/time continuum, that is the back room of the comic shop, came Anthrax, the heavy metal thrash band! Can you believe it?!

"Well, guys, what's it to be this time?"

"Well, Johnny, it's got to be 'I am the law!'"

"Alright. So, Marty, get on that record, and *hit it!*"

"15 years in the Academy, the toughest cadet they'd ever seen,

A man so hard his veins bleed ice, and when he speaks he never says it twice,

His first name is Joe, his last name is Dredd, break his law and you'll wind up dead!

His bible the book of law, its truth and justice that he's fightin' for!

Judge Dredd the man! He is the law!

Drokk it!

Respect the badge! He earned with his blood! Fear the gun!

His sentence might be death,

Because I am the law!

You aint gonna fuck around no more, I'm gonna throw away the key and lock the door!

Because I am the law!

Because I — am— the — law!"

"Okay, guys, see ya t'marra!" I said to the men of Anthrax as they vanished through the dimensional portal of the back room.

"Right, sure," Rick Munn said in rebuttal. "Judge Dredd is a faggot! He's never had sex!"

There was a deathly silence in the comic shop. No one breathed. A lone tumbleweed rolled down the street outside the window. The punters, comprising Paul Andrews, Frederick Faustenegger, Gavin Curly Hughes, Steward Reid and Marty, all took a step back towards the back of the shop.

"*What* did I hear you say?" I put my hand up to my ear in great incredulity. "Did you just call Judge Dredd a … a… " the word came out as a choke, "a homosexual?

By the holy jockstrap of Robert E. Howard, you will pay for that, hell-spawn!" I grabbed for him but he was too quick. He ran round the comic shop like a giggling wee girl, spouting more of his filth about the Judge. The chase went out the door of the shop and right into Bridge Street.

Rick Munn mockingly said, "Oh, chase me Johnny, chase me!"

"Right, that's it! You die, bastard!" I then proceeded full pelt up the street, running after him. But I was laughing too; I could see the funny side. I'm not the kind of guy who would hold a grudge for long. So, out of breath, I returned back to the comic shop. Soon after, Rick Munn returned.

"Why don't we settle this argument over a game of chess, Rick? Paul, the board!"

Paul Malone had brought his wooden chess set from his home for us to play with. Ah, the game of kings! Unbeknownst to the Munnisher, I was taking lessons from the master, Paul "The Death Bringer" Andrews. Nevertheless, I was a new crown master after beating both Pauls hands down; even Marty, despite all his cunning, could not surpass me in my hey day.

"We meet again, Obi Wan! The circle is now complete! Once I was the learner. Now I am the master!" I gloated as I began the game, doing my very best Darth Vader impression.

"Paul, the music, if you please!"

Paul had his tape deck and radio for us to listen to.

"What's it to be, Jay? Danzig?"

"But, of course, mein host! You know what I like!"

Paul inserted the cassette tape into the tape deck. The tape was *Danzig II: Lucifuge* and it had the most interesting cover design for an LP. The first track was "Long Way Back From Hell." The rough, harsh voice of Glenn Danzig filled the room, emanating from the speakers. Oh, yes! Glenn was with me that day!

"Sold into slavery down in New Orleans, Goddess of the bayou light,

Black dog's head on the killin' bed, severed and left and left to bleed,

There on fire in the corner of the world, left for God to see, there on fire in the veins of man, there in misery, there on fire in the corner of the world, left for God to see, do you wanna cross that line? Do you wanna cross that line? Do you wanna take a life?

Cause it's a long way back from Hell, and you don't no wanna go there, friend!

Poison of the human race, waiting for the bastard's son,

Malevolence sneaking up the side of the side of the world, waiting for his master's son, there on fire in the veins of man, there in misery, Lucifer's face in the mirror when you look - there for God to see!"

Rick Munn was a cunning opponent, but not cunning enough! He executed for time, for what was to be known in future as "The Munn Manoeuvre"; he gave away his Queen!

I studied the board for a moment. My eyes widened. What was he thinking? Had he seen what I had seen? Was there a trap? No! A free Queen! This was indeed an awesome sensation of victory, make no mistake! I took his Queen with grace and poise, and then chuckled most malevolently!

"Yessss!" I laughed out hard! "You see your death before you!" to voice another quote from the film, *Dune*.

"You… you… utter dirt-bag, Fisher!"

Paul Malone said, "Game over, man! Game over!"

But the Munnisher was not quite finished yet; he had a few more tricks up his sleeve, but I eventually wore him down. He fought strong and hard, though, make no mistake. A worthy opponent and then some.

"Do you know something, Johnny? Have we ever met before?"

"Now that you mention it, yeah, maybe, although I can't recall exactly when and where. You believe in reincarnation?"

"Yeah, that's it! We met in a previous lifetime!"

From that day onwards, Richard Munn and I became lifelong friends, partners in crime and fellow Astrozombies. Once the game was finished, we decided to reconcile our differences of opinion, but we all know which comic hero has chalked up the greatest number of kills in his career. The award goes to Judge Dredd for at least a count of twenty billion, and still counting — and that's just a conservative estimate!

I looked around the Outer Limits comic shop. During the months, Marty and I brought posters from home for the shop, as did all the guys. All were comic-related, and when the order from the distributors came in, we had a field day with all the publicity material, decorating our home away from home.

But there was something. I don't know, just something slightly amiss. And then it struck me. I had a vision. I would paint the door of the comic shop. I was inspired by the muse.

"Here, Paul, can I paint your back-room door with a big Judge Dredd? Brighten the place up a bit? I've got the perfect picture in the house!"

Marty said, "Go on, Paul. You should see Jay's bedroom, it's like a Judge Dredd/*2000 AD* shrine! He decorated it himself!"

Paul replied, "Well, okay, but I'll have to clear it with Robert. He owns the lease on the place, but he's slightly dubious about the last stunt you two played out the back the last time. Didn't you pair try to annexe the comic shop with the Castle Gardens?"

The back of the shop was like a wilderness. You see, the whole of Bridge Street is on a hill, with "Wicked Wendy's Soft Furnishings" (the proprietor, one

Wicked Wendy Bulldog; yes, that was her name) facing us. Yeah, she'll last long. Beside that and directly opposite was The Old Castle bar, grill and infrequent dive; going down the hill a bit there was a video shop, and above it was the Pig Farmers' Union, oink, oink. How bizarre. But let us proceed on.

We were talking about the back of the comic shop. As I was saying, it was a like a jungle out the back, and Marty and I hacked our way through and up the steep rise to Castle Gardens. I forget some of my local history, but Lisburn has always been a garrison town, full of walls and barricades, shit like that; hence the need to destroy and deface such things, like all teenagers from Mars. We faced our enemy. It was a daunting task, and then some. Marty kept muttering under his breath,

"Know your enemy, Johnny, know your enemy…"

"And it would've succeeded, too, if it hadn't have been for those pesky spoons breaking on the walls while we dug!" Marty chuckled heartily.

"You should have seen the look on Gary's face! He was totally livid with shock when he saw what you were up to!" Paul exclaimed.

"Anyway, umm, aren't the walls at Castle Gardens meant to be listed buildings or such like?" he added.

"So what? We don't give a flying frag, do we, Marty?" I asked my companion.

Marty nodded in agreement.

I added, "So, that's sorted. I'll do the door."

And I did the door and it stood there in all its glory, guarding the shop and the back room for nigh on four years. The stern image of Justice, the Judge Dredd, holding a dead punk in his left hand, with his raised Lawgiver in his right hand.

Jonathan, aged 19, painting door of Outer Limits with Gavin Curly Hughes, Paddy and Paul

In Outer Limits
Left to right: Jonathan, aged 24, Paul Malone, Judge Dredd, Robert Malone and Stephen Bent

Alison Møller - she is the sister of Marty and Keith

CHAPTER TEN: GLORY AND GORY DAYS

The years between 1989 and 1992 were my golden and glory years. I fell in love twice and had glorious sex on numerous occasions and in various locations (as you do).

In the spring of 1989, I met Ellen Scramble in an old folks' hospital where I was doing some work for Voluntary Services, Lisburn. It was love at first sight. When I introduced her to the guys at the shop, Marty diagnosed her as "mad as a brush!" But I didn't care. She had a great body and then some.

Anyway, long before Wayne had his little World and long before Bill and Ted had their excellent adventures, there was the original: The John Fisher Radio Show, hosted by the man with the most, yours truly. It was me, broadcast from a top-secret location, somewhere in the Lisburn area. Okay, a friend of Marty's had a large Citizen Band antenna, from which he broadcast at one of the highest frequencies available. He was one of these "Radio Hams" you hear about.

The frequency was 108 megahertz and the station was aptly named Hiss FM. We broadcast all over Western Europe and beyond — Moira, that is, and because the frequency was so high, we had a little bother from the authorities. Subsequently, I dedicated a song to the brave boys up at Thiepval Barracks who, I believe, monitor most, if not all, of the traffic on the airwaves with their early warning radar for

"The Big One," ie World War Three. I remember one day, Marty told me that, once upon a time, when there was a power cut he had told his wee kid sister, Ally, that the nukes were coming for her because of the electro magnetic pulse, which is associated with a nuclear detonation, causing massive power failures all over the country. The poor kid bawled her wee eyes out. No wonder Marty wanted to be a dentist. He had a wicked, yet almost vicious streak of humour, just like me.

So, there we were. We even had jingles and advertisements! A good friend of Rick, Marty and Paddy supplied them. His name was Jason "Jakey" Reilly, to give the guy his credit. He had an eight-track mixing machine in his mate's garage on which he produced his jingles for us. It's amazing what an electric guitar, an echo pedal, rock and roll attitude, and a drum kit can produce. Jake Reilly did the intro sequence for me to "Cosmic Fact" and the "Culture Shock" jingles. A mate of Marty did another jingle for the show. It was a bit like the Blues Brothers intro and it went something like this. Voice-over,

"*Good evening, ladies and gentlemen,*" (trumpets and blues with a large crowd cheering effect), "*welcome to the Jonathan Fisher Radio show. May I say how privileged you are to be listening tonight. So, for the blues shoes and whatever else rhymes, tune in every Tuesday night at 5pm for the Jonathan Fisher Radio show*" (triumphant saxophone and horn solos with cheering crowds fading away into the distance).

That one was one of my favourites, and was well-liked by a few of the guys down in the shop — but that was just the thin edge of the wedge.

Now for my introduction jingle, which began something like this: a single guitar melody, playing a gentle soothing tune, and the voice-over said in a mild tone,

"Hiss FM proudly presents…" (suddenly the guitar ripped into a heavy metal rift, pumping out pure energy and sound, and then the voice was almost screaming!)

"The John Fisher Radio Show!" and I said,

"*Yeah!*" and the voice continued to scream.

"One hundred and eight megahertz in the Lisburn area — listen or die!"

Then it was time for my spiel.

"You'd better believe it! Here's your host, the man with the most, here'ssss Johnny!" All the time, the heavy metal music roared in the background. I said enthusiastically,

"Tonight we are packed full with adventure, excitement, and really wild things, including all your favourites: Stan Ridgeway, The Count, err, Sebastian and his little dog and of course, Marty!"

At this point, I handed the microphone over to Marty as quickly as I could, and he said,

"Also on tonight's show, we have, umm, Zappa, Frank Zappa, and some tracks from our session band, "The Afterbirth Boys." These tracks are exclusively recorded for our show, and won't be heard anywhere else. Alan … "

Marty handed the mike to Alan McColonicIrrigation. For the record, I never liked the guy, nor trusted him. He was Marty's school buddy and he was secretly porking Paul Malone's girlfriend, Aynat, behind Paul's back, although we didn't know about this at the time! The guy was only good for a dogsbody; changing records, stuff like that.

Alan squeaked,

"We'll also have interviews with Glenn Danzig, lead vocalist of the Misfits, Samhain, and his new band Danzig. We'll have some tracks by Iron Maiden, The Electro-hippies, and many, many more. Johnny … "

"Thanks. I'd like to thank Jakey Reilly for his totally awesome new vamped tunes, totally awesome, man! I'd also like to say 'Hi' to Jason Paul, in his awesome Volkswagen of Doom! Oh, the first track coming up: this is Frank Zappa, 'Stick It Out'. So, Marty, get on that record and hit it!"

The intro music faded, and it was just a perfect link and join to the record, as Marty put the record on the turntable. The rest, as the old saying goes, is history!

After the first song played, we were on a roll. We were hot, so hot we were smokin'! During the first sketch, Marty had these small excerpts from some of his and my favourite television series recorded onto audio tape: *Blackadder, The Prisoner,*

Star Trek, things like that. So, it went like this.

"We want information... information... information!"

"Who are you? The John Fisher Radio Show!"

"Who is Number One? We are!"

"You... are Number Six! No, man —that's Steve Write!"

"I am not a number: I am a free man! You'd better believe it! This is the John Fisher Radio Show, and our next track is "Shy Boy" by David Lee Roth. So, hit it!"

During that spring and summer we did at least ten episodes of the John Fisher Radio Show, maybe a bit closer to fifteen and then some. Marty went to Austria for his holidays that summer, and he swears he picked us up on his radio but the Austrian/Germans called it Der Johann Fischer Radio Blitzkrieg.

"Vorsprung durch Technik", as they say in Lisburn.

CHAPTER ELEVEN: TITCH FISHER

I killed our dog.

I loved the tiny creature more than anyone else in the world, at that time, at least. We were a bit like that film, *Old Yeller*. She grew up with the whole family. For fourteen years, she was our pole star, a constant thing in our lives. But I killed my dog.

She started to haemorrhage inside, but we didn't know until she started showing the same symptoms as Kerry, our other dog. Remember?

This time, I decided not to bring her down to Archbold. No, this time, I took her down to the vets on Union Bridge, holding her in my small holdall bag. I knew she couldn't walk that distance. I went with Rick Black in his car.

I asked the vet to examine her. He recommended a hysterectomy, but advised that she might not survive the operation. There was a chance of less than fifty-fifty. The decision was left to me. It was mine and mine alone. I looked at the vet, at his girly receptionist. They looked at me. I looked at Titch. The wee dog looked almost comical, sitting in that wee bag, but this was no joke. This was reality in its most brutal form. I thought back to how Kerry had suffered, and I decided. God, forgive me. I shut my eyes and ordered an execution. Euthanasia on order.

I held my dog, my precious Chien, in my arms. I assured her it was going to be all right. She nuzzled up to me. Her wee nose was dry and warm. I held Titch for one last time as a living, breathing being. I held back fiery red tears — I watched as the vet inserted the needle into her paw, and I watched as the pump squeezed inwards. My wee dog went limp, like a sack of potatoes. She shuddered once and died. I killed my dog.

Close your eyes, Titch, please, I thought to myself, but I had to close them for her. As I lifted her from the bench, her wee tongue popped out from her wee mouth. It was still warm. Why didn't you scream out loud, Titch? But she hadn't. She just went to sleep, in a way.

I threw blood money at the vet, put my dog into my bag, and zipped it shut. I left the abattoir.

Rick got me home without a word. I thanked him for doing this for me. I ran through our front door, right into the arms of my mother and father. I couldn't contain myself. The floodgates opened and it all came rushing out like a flood of grief and self-loathing. I killed my dog.

I buried her in her favourite spot in the garden where she used to lie in the summer months.

My father had been right. Happiness was dog-shaped.

Chapter Twelve: Crazy

I really wasn't in the mood to go up the Mourne Mountains, what with Titch's death still in my thoughts. But, what the hell! It would be an adventure.

Or so I thought.

I thought I would get away from civilisation with one's girlfriend. Who knows what mischief we could get up to — if she was prepared, that is. She assured me that she was. How wrong could I have been?

It was the weekend when the "Glorious Twelfth" was celebrated throughout the land. Well, Northern Ireland. Robert Malone drove us to the entrance of Tullymore Forest Park in the smallest car on the Earth, or so it seemed at that time — a Fiat Panda. On board was Paul Malone, Heather Hamilton (Paul's new squeeze, otherwise known as HH), and myself and my crazy Ellen, not to mention all our gear. We were packed in there like a tin of Arcturian mega sardines, and, boy, that was tight! HH was an attractive hippy-chick with long, curly black hair and piercing blue eyes. A marked difference to the evil Aynat Bubezleeb, whose current whereabouts were Alan McColonicIrrigation's face, no doubt. Anyway, we got unloaded and said goodbye to Bob Malone. I was prepared, ready to hit that mountain! I had with me my TA training, my boots and my good old rucksack, in which was my two-man tent, otherwise known as my intended man-on-woman shagging base. I had all I needed:

Check.

Paul and Heather were also ready; they had a real fancy high-tech sex tent. Double-check.

Crazy Ellen. I could not believe it! She had brought with her a tiny wee handbag in which she only had her fraggin' high-heeled shoes and a white lab coat from work! Why!? I was so mad at her! She had come totally unprepared.

"Ellen," I said quietly, "did you bring the prima-stove and the tin-opener like you said you would?"

"No," she replied innocently.

"Don't talk that nonsense with me, wench! You know you were meant to!" I said in frustration and anger — I nearly blew a fuse! I turned to Paul in disgust, asked him if I could use their stove and asked whether he had a tin-opener.

"No worries, Jay."

Then I asked her coldly, "What have you got to wear on your feet?"

"Oh," she giggled, like it was some kind of game, throwing her hair over her shoulder. "These!"

From her bag, she produced a pair of gutties. Paul and Heather rolled their eyes in disbelief.

"Well, they will have to do you," I said even more coldly. "Okay, Paul, lead the way, man."

It was all so surreal it was unreal and the journey had only just begun.

It was easygoing for the first few miles, as we kept to the dirt tracks of the forest. However, things became progressively worse as we began to lose sight of the track with the fading light. To add to our misfortunes, we had to trek though a prehistoric jungle of waist-high ferns, which hindered our progress. It was like something from a scene of that famous Nam film, *Apocalypse Now*. We were uncertain of our footing in the dense foliage, with deep gullies to the left of us, and, even worse, to the right of me was my Ellen.

Ellen, with her cheery as Shirley Temple on acid "On The Good Ship Lollypop" attitude and her skipping, prancing, whistling and wanting us all to join in, was starting to bite. *[Jay Note: Young Shirley was a child movie-star in the 1930s, infamous for the song in question.]* This was fine for her as she wasn't laden down with a one hundred pound rucksack, or so it felt to me.

We finally caught sight of a suitable flat bit of ground in the pit, located down one of the gullies on the left side of one of the lesser mountains, Slieve Commedagh, I think it was. It was getting misty and the temperature was beginning to drop, and so we decided to make camp. I tried to put my tent up, but Ellen had other ideas. She decided to abandon me in preference to washing her feet in a small stream by the campsite. At that moment, I felt like the loneliest guy on Earth because I was still upset about my dog Titch. I thought to myself,

What the hell am I doing here, far from my family with this crazy mad-as-a-brush girl, trying in vain to climb a mountain? Adding to the misery was the local midge-fly population — the bastards. I hate those wee fraggers. They were everywhere, bloody millions of them and they bite and bite hard.

Come to think of it, I don't know what was worse: Ellen or the gnats.

Heather and Paul had their own tent up in what seemed like seconds, but I was still struggling with mine and Ellen was nowhere to be seen. Paul and Heather wanted to help me with my rubbish two-man tent, or one-man one-womanless tent, but I was too pig-headed and stubborn to accept their help. That was her job.

Where the fraggin' hell is she? I thought. At one point, I just didn't give a flying frag about her; I just wanted to get into the relative safety of my tent.

"It's up!" I finally rejoiced. Oh come on, reader. I meant the tent.

I called for her.

No answer, and now the search began for the missing wench.

When I did eventually find her, I found out that she had first gone and washed her feet (like some late-day pilgrim, 'get off your horse and drink your milk') and then gone snooping around Paul and Heather! Later, when I interrogated her, I found out that she liked the look of Paul's Shag Master 3000 (which was actually Heather's tent) and was looking for a room at the inn! I wasn't too pleased about that, putting it mildly. Dear Ellen apparently felt that my tent, the Dew Master AD 150, which had stood me the test of time all these years, was not to her liking, nor to her bloody standards. I felt like going Captain Caveman on her (but that was soon to come), clubbing her around the head and dragging her back to my mobile hobbit hole, cave even.

At last I crawled inside the tent, exhausted and still angry, but that was about to fade. With a gleam in my eye and a full-on robot chubby in my pants (thanks, Bill and Ted), I soon forgave her and quickly got on with the business at hand of pleasing myself and, to be honest, without much concern for her feelings.

[Jay Note: the "full-on robot chubby" as used by the characters Bill and Ted in the movie Bill and Ted's Bogus Journey, 1991.]

When I look back in hindsight, I feel regret and some shame at the way I treated her. I know it's no excuse but I was young and foolish at the time. We both were.

"Wham, bam, thank you, ma'am."

With my passion spent, Ellen turned to me and said,

"Jonathan, why are these flies in the tent? We're being eaten alive here!"

"Well I'm not God or Moses controlling the plagues and you're the one that didn't pack the insect repellent. I mean, you hardly packed anything!"

She just gave a mere shrug of the shoulders and turned away from me indignantly.

The night passed slowly and I could hear only the moaning of the wind and Ellen, the gnats buzzing, and Paul and Heather shagging in their tent. Ellen essentially still wanted to sly off to the safety of the Shag Master 3000 — but I was not having any of that! No way, José!

At that time, I was jealous and too proud to go looking for help from Paul and Heather. I considered Paul to be the alpha male in our group and I looked up to him for his worldly wisdom. In addition, I didn't want Paul to get near my female. Not that I didn't trust Paul — I did — but I just wanted her all to myself.

Ellen and I didn't get any sleep that night, basically because of a combination of the fight we had, the cold, and being constantly harassed by the feckin' flies. I was utterly peeved off with the entire situation. I just wanted to be home, safe and warm. It was to turn out to be a pure hell-trek.

After a lifelong night, dawn broke over the Mournes. It was a damp, grey morning with a light mist hanging in the air, which was burning off pretty quickly in the morning sun. I can't recall much of that morning, but suffice it to say I was cold, fecked off, and hungry. I got up to fix breakfast and found Ellen's shoes outside the tent, soaking wet.

Just another day in Paradise, I thought to myself.

After time, everyone had got up and had breakfast, and then we started to break camp for our first day in the forest. We struggled for higher ground, to get away from the bastard gnats. It was heavy going, as I had brought along tinned food, TA rations and some high-calorie sweets, which were Vitamin C-enriched, to suck on whilst we marched up Slieve Donard. Our only hindrance was Ellen.

It was late afternoon, when we saw other climbers on the path up the mountain, and others coming down. We noticed a couple of kids hiking, a boy and an older girl, going up the mountain by themselves.

I went up the Mournes with Ellen, well to get jiggy with it. Hell, I guess every guy in the world would climb any mountain to experience that feeling of love. Phallic symbolism aside, and all that Freudian bull, I thought I loved her. But, at the end, it was just, well, sexual attraction I suppose.

By early evening we had climbed about three-quarters of the way up the mountain and we pitched camp for the night by a stream. As the stars were coming out, the mountains were shrouded in mist and the stillness of that scene ranks as one of the most breathtaking sights in my life. (I won't sing Percy French here, even though I was tempted to.) Far below was the town of Newcastle.

There were three guys with booze pitched in a tent across the stream from us, and Ellen made a beeline for them, waving her breasts about. I said to myself with a knot in my stomach, God, no. Where the hell does she think she's going now? I tried to pull her back, but it was too damn late — the damage was done.

I remember once watching on television, and later reading, Ray Bradbury's "The Martian Chronicles", in which the Earth men pollute a Martian stream with beer. Now, as much as that place wasn't Mars, the similes were the same, as was the disgust I felt.

"Hello, boys!" Ellen tittered (Yet another breast joke! Boom, boom, there I go again!). She giggled.

In different circumstances, these guys would have been a welcome diversion. Their names were Tom, Dick and Harry. They knew every *Blackadder* sketch under the sun, and they worked in the Wellworths store in Newcastle. They were lounging about drinking, with their hands behind their backs.

"You have a woman's purse, my Lord!" They all guffawed as Ellen came closer. They continued, "I wager that dainty purse has never been used to plug the hole in a breach."

"And what's your name, my pretty?" Dick asked.

"Oh, my name is Ellen, and this is my boyfriend Jonathan, and they're Paul and Heather, our friends."

They nodded to Paul and Heather.

Tommy said, "Do ya fancy drink?"

"Sorry, no thanks," I said politely.

"Come, wench." I took Ellen firmly by the arm. "It's time to get unpacked and put my supper on!"

"Suit yourself," Harry replied.

We started a campfire from brushwood we found nearby to warm us all. It was getting dark. In our tent, we had a heavy petting session. Afterwards, I told her to go to sleep. I put a veil over that incident.

I was a real bastard. I'd had quite enough of her whining for one day and I was in no mood.

Mental note to self, I thought sleepily. Dump Ellen at first available opportunity.

Unfortunately, my well-earned rest was short-lived. From outside, I heard screams. At first, I thought it was Heather and Paul 'at it' again, but that was not the case this time. No, the screams were distant, but coming closer. I hurriedly shoved my boots on and leapt out of the tent, leaving Ellen sleeping fitfully. I raised the alarm at the other tent, vigorously shaking the tent pole.

Paul looked out, somewhat bemused.

I said, "C'mon, man, d'ya hear that?"

Heather looked out. "What's happening, Jay?"

The screams were almost on top of us. Paul and I went out to see where the shouts were coming from. I told Heather to look on Ellen and see if she was okay.

In the pale moonlight, we could see two figures stumbling in the darkness. I bounded across the stream. Paul was not far behind.

He said, *"Holy fuck!"* He saw me leaping like a salmon, not believing what I'd just done. We both raced up the mountain path.

"Help! Oh, help us!" It was the two children we had passed on the way up the mountain. They were in a terrible state, in shock, no doubt. I took the girl's hand, Paul took the hand of the boy and we led them both down to our camp.

"Oh, thank you, mister!" The girl said, looking up at me adoringly and holding my hand in a vice-like grip!

By the time we got back, there was the question of who was going to look after them. Heather was the obvious choice. Her maternal instincts surfaced. She got them a warm cup of tea and a snack.

"There, there. You are safe now," she said reassuringly. Heather pulled me to one side for a moment, her curling hair blowing in the sea wind, the embers of the dying campfire catching her eyes as they sparked intelligently. She said,

"You know something, Jay? The girl, Jane, is there something wrong with her?"

The boy John came over and added,

"Oh, aye, she has fits or something."

Fan-bloody-tastic — that was all we needed.

Eventually, we got them into Paul and Heather's tent. I tried to resume sleep, but we were, again, caught short.

"Hell's bells!"

From out of the darkness and now heading up the mountain was the entire local search and rescue party! Search lights, sniffer dogs, people, medics, and stretchers — the works! We handed Jane and John over to the authorities, assuming that their parents had raised the alarm.

"Good work, guys," one of the rescue team said.

"No problem," Paul said, shrugging off the praise. "Anyone in the same circumstances would've done the same thing."

"Nonetheless, it was a brave thing you did." The man turned to me. "What's your name?" he asked, nodding his head in my direction.

I looked at Paul, knowing he was thinking the same thoughts as I was.

"We don't want any publicity — but thanks all the same."

The girl, Jane, looked back at me fondly as she left. And for the record, a backward glance is always a good thing. My hero!

The following morning we left the Mournes and went down to Newcastle. Ellen had arranged for her boss at the chemist's to pick her up and take her to Lisburn. I knew I had to go with her — I was duty-bound.

"Look guys," I said sadly. "I have to go. When I pick up my bike I'll tell Bob to lift you guys up. I'm so sorry, man."

"Never again, Robert. Never again, Bob!" I said, shaking my head despondently.

It was early morning when I buzzed for Bob Malone. My code was two short buzzes followed by a longer buzz. Robert had actually bought the holy premises of 47 Bridge Street, using his photography business as his sideline. That was his excuse, at least, but we all knew Robert's seedier past. He had done some work for a jazz mag.

"Yeah, I know I was young and foolish. So was my 'model', or something along those lines." But anyway, still yawning, Robert opened the gates of Outer Limits to admit me into his inner sanctum.

He came to his door wearing a shirt, jeans, socks and glasses.

"Oh, good morning," he yawned, taking off his glasses, scratching himself where only men can.

"Jay, how was the trip?" He put his glasses back on and rubbed his roughened stubble chin and looked at me through blurred eyed.

His eyes widened and his jaw dropped when I told what had transpired.

Robert exclaimed, "Oh. Well. Fuck. Sorry, man."

"My sentiments exactly, Robert. Can you believe that crazy woman?!" As I spoke, I realised I was still furious with her.

"Do you mind if I leave my tent and gear in the back, Bob?" I sighed and shook my head.

"Never again!"

In Mega City
Left to right: Jonathan, Simon Bisley and Pat Mills

CHAPTER THIRTEEN: UNLUCKY FOR SOME

We were on a mission; a mission from God — well, from the Outer Limits comic shop, actually, but what the heck! The comic shop was like the almighty in those days.

With *Marvel* filth on one side and *DC Comics* on the other, I worshipped the shrine that was *2000 AD* right at the back. Whilst browsing on my knees, like a light of sunshine I happened to see an advert in the prog. I stood up from my prayers. With the Hallelujah chorus ringing in my ears, I showed it to the guys in the comic shop.

"Holy Drokk!" I exclaimed to Paul. "Look at this, matey!" It was a *Slaine* signing session with Pat Mills and Simon Bisley at Mega City comic shop in London. For the uninitiated, Slaine was a Celtic Barbarian character created by Pat and Angie Mills for a sword and sorcery epic for the *2000 AD* comic. On this occasion, a signing session would have countless boy and girl fans attending to have their comics or graphic novels signed by their demigods — the writers and artists.

Holy frag, I wistfully mused to myself, and said, "Boy, wouldn't it be totally awesome if we could go?"

"Well, why not Jay, my best buddy? We could! I won some holiday vouchers a while back; they need using!"

So there was the mission and we gleefully accepted it.

We had to assemble our team of Fan Boys for this holy of holiest quests. There was Paul the Crom-Meister Malone with his Frank Frazetta fetish, comic lord of all he surveyed, and then some, and my best friend to boot, who also had paid for Robert's ticket, as well as mine, with the holiday vouchers he had won. (It was a bit like the golden ticket in *Charlie and the Chocolate Factory* for me!). Robert was essential for our purposes as the team, erm, cough, pornographer (photographer). I wanted Marty Møller to go with us but, unfortunately, he was on a Duke of Edinburgh Award scheme and couldn't come. Then there was oily rat-features McColonicIrrigation who had bought a ticket from his schoolmistress. Yeah, I wonder what sort of after-school shenanigans he had to perform to get that one, eh?! I bet I can state with all certainty that it wasn't banging dusters together! Or was it? Dun dun daaa!

Alan had conducted the most evil of sins possible and Paul was our hero and target. There should have been a sign outside the door of the comic shop (instead of "Abandon all hope, all ye who enter here") — the eleventh commandment,

"Thou shalt not pork or sniff round thy best friend's girlfriend or woman." Then there was me, Jonathan Fisher, Team Leader, *2000 AD*, number one fan boy extreme. There was nothing to stop us now!

We planned our strike force to hit London from the Malone residence. We packed progs, *Slaine* graphic novels, *A.B.C. Warriors*, the whole works for the dynamic duo to sign. Before we set off, however, there was one last duty to be performed: the watching of the *Blues Brothers* on Gary Malone's VCR, from which we took our inspiration for our trip amongst trips!

I had to tell my parents the truth — not. I knew they would only worry about me, and so I was forced, shackled and gagged, to tell my Mum a tiny white lie.

"Mummy, don't worry, the guys and I are going to stay in the YMCA in

London. Failing that, we'll rent a hostel or something! Don't worry! I'll be fine! I'll phone you when I get home!" I hugged and kissed her on the cheek.

And then, we were off!

To the International Airport we went, travelling in Robert's white Panda car. With rucksacks on our backs, which were full to bursting with comics, we had only the clothes on our backs and no room for essentials. Yep, lacking in the "clean underwear" department — at least some of us were. Me? Well, as my mother always says,

"Always wear clean underwear, Jonathan, you never know!" Yes, and dear old mummy is right (as mothers inevitably are). Yes, I know where she's coming from. You could get into an accident or a life-threatening situation, and the horror could just unfold whereby you evacuate your bowels or, as is more commonly known, you shit yourself. Anyway.

I really enjoy flying. Paul warned me to take some barley sugar to suck on so that my ears wouldn't pop or explode or some other such horrific event. I got the window seat beside Paul, and Alan and Robert took the opposite aisle.

We were served food by a male steward/cabin boy, whatever the correct term is these days and depending on which ocean you happen to be flying over.

"Would you gentlemen care for a drink?" he said in a high-pitched feminine voice.

Soon, we were flying high amongst the clouds over the Irish Sea to England, nonchalantly sipping our drinks. It was a thrilling experience for me, seeing the world from the economy class seats; it was truly remarkable and cheap! But, that was our style, and you'd better believe it, baby!

After around forty-five minutes, we finally saw from our view-ports the magnificent sight of London. I could see Battersea's famous power station towers, the Queen's residence, Hyde Park, Tower Bridge, HMS Belfast and the Thames Barricade! It was totally fraggin' awesome!

Yes, dear reader. The Fisher had arrived! Methinks it's high time for a song, so here goes London Dungeon by none other than Glenn Danzig and The Misfits!

"They called us walking corpses, unholy living dead!

They had to lock us up, put us in their British Hell!

Make sure your face is clean boy — can't have no dirty dead!

All the corpses here are clean boy, all the Yanks in British Hell!

I don't wanna be here in your London Dungeon,

Ain't no mystery why am in misery — it's Hell!"

London is, undoubtedly, my kinda town! Old Smoky, Londinium, the capital of the United Kingdom. Ladies of London, beware! The guys are in town! Mothers, lock up your daughters — the Celts are coming!

At the airport, we were unsure how much the tickets were for the tube, but the ticket clerk gave us a "tourist/sightseeing deal" for the princely sum of two pounds fifty. Bargain. That gave us the full scope for the whole tube network! Anyway, we took the tube from Heathrow Airport and travelled into the centre of London town.

We were like a bunch of school kids on a day out, all hyper and full of adrenaline.

En route, we sat talking amongst ourselves, minding our own sightseeing business, when a rather peculiar young man, dressed in a dinner suit, holding a silver cane (with, I might add, a bulldog at its head), and — I kid you not — wearing a magician's cape entered our carriage accompanied by his lady friend. He stood and introduced himself to us.

"I am Julian Peabody, and this is my assistant Gertrude Yagbottom, and we," he nodded to his gorgeous companion, "are here to entertain you all!"

What happened next was the most bizarre song and dance duet I had ever witnessed. It was a cross between "The Good Ship Lollypop" and Fred Astaire and Ginger Rodgers on acid, and *West Side Story*!

We had our mouths open in awe and agog.

"Remember my name, good folk: the name's Peabody, Julian Peabody." He added when the routine was over, "I will be the first gay Prime Minister of this fair land, and I bid you all farewell and adieu!" He turned away, slinging his cape over his shoulder like Béla Lugosi would have done. He departed at the next stop, with Gertrude trailing close behind.

I clapped in admiration. I was tempted to wolf-whistle, but I didn't want to make that sort of impression.

We left the tube at Oxford Street and headed into the jostling crowds. We saw millions of people thronging their way through the streets of London town. Truly, this was a mega city. Paul led us down Oxford Street and we began heading towards the heart of the capital.

With excitement buzzing through my veins, I couldn't help but feel a wave of sadness as I acknowledged the people's blank expressions as they journeyed through the amazing streets. Same old same all over the world.

We strolled along the Thames embankment and towards Cleopatra's Needle (ouch). We took photographs acting the fool at Big Ben, and then we headed into the Forbidden Planet! Sure, it was all swanky, what with the old comics of *Spiderman, issue one, Action Comics Superman*, and the holy grail of all comics — *Batman*. But did they have what we had in Outer Limits? No, sir! We had the Bat Bowl! In the bowels of Outer Limits, right at the back of the shop where few feared to tread, and carefully they did. Basically, the room was dark, dank, with a turnip smell of joss sticks and a single bulb hanging in the dark air, wherein I attempted to build a four-dimensional hyper cube with straws from Burger Ming. *[Jay Note: I loved the Carl Sagan book, Cosmos. From the pages of said book I was inspired to build a hyper cube.]*

I had gone down to the local Burger Ming and liberated a humongous amount of straws from the pretty, blonde, serving wench at the front, who asked with her eyes opened wide,

"May I help you?"

"No," I replied as a matter of fact, shaking my head.

Subsequently, I unsuccessfully tried to hypnotise Paul Andrews, the "Death Bringer," using a small torch, attempting to steer him away from his nicotine addiction. I placed him in the dark, sitting on the Bat Bowl, seat down of course! I intoned with my mantra:

"Smoking kills! Smoking kills! Smoking kills!" as I waved my torch in front of him. Alas, my experiment was doomed. He was cured for point zero zero seven of a nanosecond.

The Bat Bowl was located in the toilet, err, area. Basically, I had pasted on the cistern a Batman image, who was in the throes of pooping, a speech bubble shouting out, "Holy crap, Batman, must — force — it — out!"

There was one other piece of equipment — the Kettle from Hell. This was used to brew tea for us in the shop; it had other uses, however…

One time, Mark Freeman, a veteran of the first Gulf War and one of our fellow comic shop illuminati, had come down to see Paul in the shop. We were all chatting, standing round the desk and playing chess, when we got onto the subject of food.

Mark said, "You know, lads, I haven't had a Farley's Rusk in years!" His stomach growled in anticipation and hunger, as he folded his arms and stroked his chin.

We all agreed Farley's Rusks was the food of the gods, from the sweet ambrosia taste to the texture. We all hankered for the strange infantile fulfilment. And so I rushed down to Greanz food store — and thus it was! *[Jay Note: Greanz food store was situated in the middle of Lisburn and Zombie Central for all the oldsters.]*

"Paul!" I shouted upon my return. "Do you have a saucepan for the milk?" I

Mark Freeman

raised my eyebrows.

Paul frowned, adjusted his glasses from his nose, took them off and polished them on his woolly polo-neck jumper and replaced them.

"No, Jay. Sorry, I don't!"

We all looked at the kettle.

"Why don't we use the kettle?" We all said in unison. It was a complete eureka moment.

So, in good nature, Paul filled the kettle with milk and set it to boil. The feast was set to begin! We all grabbed a mighty mug each and proceeded to dish out the milky goodness. Ah, the teats of the cow!

"Oh, man," I enthused as the warmth trickled down my throat. "This is the best! You can't get much better!" The room was filled with milky steam wafting through the air.

Paul and Mark nodded in agreement.

Mark added, "Adapt, survive and overcome! Hoorah!"

We all laughed out loud, our bellies full of those amazing rusks from the Farley gods.

The following morning, I cycled from my house and down to the comic shop where I would usually park my bike at the back of Outer Limits store. And that was where Gary Malone made the grim discovery…

"Jay?" Gary exclaimed, "What the fornication happened to the kettle? I tried to make a cuppa…" His voice trailed off, "and this came out!"

It was disgusting — that was one word for it. The milk had congealed on the kettle's filaments and, as a result, anytime we tried to boil water afterwards culminated in little success.

Marty Møller came in and piped up, "Johnny, that looks like after-birth!"

So, the kettle was officially named redundant but we all still made tea from it. Honestly, we had little choice in the matter. It was either that or the dreaded tap water.

To continue, we had lunch at Wimpy and this was my virgin burger. I had refused the temptations of Burger Ming and Big Sac back in ye olde Lisburn. Here, however, I had decided to go Regal! Well, when in Rome, do as the Romans do. Alan had suggested it. My choice of meal and, as we were on a tight budget…

Afterwards, it was time for a little sightseeing. Robert Malone was team photographer and he happily snapped us at Big Ben, at the BBC Broadcasting Corporation (oh yes, it will be mine one day), and in Trafalgar Square where I climbed up and onto the lion's rump where

"We came, we saw, we conquered."
Jonathan, Paul and Alan at Nelson's Column. Jonathan and the lion.
Alan, Paul and Jonathan outside Buckingham Palace. Alan, Paul and Jonathan outside the café.

I joyfully sat. By this point, I was knackered from walking round London. Robert took an amazing atmospheric photograph of me sitting there. We had made a banner which Paul airbrushed with "OUTER LIMITS", which we unfurled at the base of Nelson's Column and aptly depicted the struggle of the sea battle of Trafalgar. We struck heroic poses there, with myself at the front, Paul in the middle and Alan at the other end, furthest away from me — the specimen.

Chinatown rocked. We loved the smells and sights. We checked out Soho with other delights — briefly. The light was fading and the street lamps began to switch on, and so we moved swiftly away. The scene was, disappointingly, not quite Mary Poppins. I had imagined it to be something like Dick van Dyke, complete with cheeriness, ye olde street lamps and London fogs, guv'nor. Instead, yet another childhood fantasy was dispelled. Damn you, Dick Whittington! Sadly, there were no chimney sweeps to be seen plying their trade. Of course, there were other characters plying other trades, but more on this later.

Euston station; the place was huge. We decided to head into the shops and look around a little. A little while later, it was late and we were tired, and so we decided to find a quiet area to lay down our sleeping bags. Beginning to yawn sleepily we all picked a nice spot beneath a huge hexagon to stretch out our weary limbs. We saw one guy dressed in a sharp suit, complete with gold cuff-links, watch and tie, sleeping in a photo booth and there was a tall, thin black dude shouting at the top off his voice,

"Southern hospitality? Kiss my brown bottom!" as he walked to and fro!

A few other commuters passed us. There was one stunning black girl and she was drop-dead gorgeous. I was stunned, honestly and completely. I said (or shouted rather),

"Hey! Would you marry me? Take me home?" She simply smiled and giggled to her companion before moving on out of my life forever. Ah, well. C'est la vie.

We can pick them, let me tell you. To further expand our already-bursting portfolio of weirdos — in the comic shop we had a string of them — complete Neanderthals, cheese rangers, various anorak-wearing geeks and frakazoids, but there was this one guy who took the proverbial biscuit. Robert christened him "Cat Weasel."

Cat Weasel looked like as you'd expect. He had curly, dark blonde hair with a long, curly beard and was possibly lice-infected, hair and beard both. While we were lying in the station, minding our own business, he came up to us and sat down, lotus position upwind, so that we could fully and completely appreciate the true glory of his stench.

"Paul?" I gagged, choking slightly. "Who is this guy?" My eyes began to water; he smelled like warm dog food — or maybe even dog's produce from the opposite end.

Cat Weasel started talking to Bob.

"Hey, man. Have you got any?" he said in a low mumble. "I had sex with Annie Lennox, you know, man. Yeah, for sure. She was hot." His voice trailed off and he started saying random words like pixie, lobster in the sea, Bruce Forsythe, I know Elvis, man, I fought in the Trojan War with Achilles, orange stars.

We all inched our sleeping bags away like four caterpillars and, as luck would genuinely have it this time around, we were asked by the police to leave, giving us the perfect excuse to bolt from our stinky friend. Some of us had been sleeping fitfully when the dirty oinkers had kicked Robert's sleeping bag.

"Hello lads," one officer said to us. "What's all this then?"

I had never seen a London bobby before. I was tempted to call him "tit head", but I knew that would have us in the back of the Black Maria and on the way to New Scotland Yard for sure. I could see the headlines in the Sunday papers screaming, "Four Northern Irish men verbally assault brave bobby." Quite simply, we didn't have a leg to stand on, figuratively speaking that is, and we knew it. We also had no place to stay the night and so we wandered through the dark streets of London until we finally reached King's Cross and an all-night café called The Purple Parrot.

Mmmm, I mused to myself. I wonder why it's called that? And, before any of you unsympathetic readers laugh at my expense, let me just say: I was nineteen, fresh-faced and very naive.

Outside, there were loads of men smoking, all striking poses, complete with handlebar moustaches, leather jackets and small German captain hats titled to one side. Inside the establishment there was more of the same, significantly more, in actual fact.

"What'll it be fellas?" said the proprietor of the Parrot in a gruff voice, eyeing us up whilst polishing up a teacup with a towel.

"Four teas please," said Alan.

"Certainly, young man," replied the owner with a strange smile spreading across his goatee beard.

We all sat down, and the tea was served. I spotted a sign on the wall.

"Guys!" I indicated to Paul and Robert, "we can stay the night! It says that room's got half-hour rents!"

Robert choked on his tea when he read the sign.

"Drink up, Jay," he spluttered. "Just drink up. We're leaving now!" We all turned in unison, scraping the chairs behind us. And it was then that we saw the leather trousers of the owner, without any backside in his pants. He just had a hairy arse.

To say we couldn't get out any quicker is a significant understatement.

By this point, it was around half three in the morning, and so we decided to risk going back to the station. Thankfully, there were no police and, even more thankfully, no Cat Weasel, and so we managed to hunker down till morning.

All too soon, Sunday morning in London town arose. This was it! The culmination, the climax of our journey to meet Pat Mills again! We knew our day was set to be full of adventure of the highest kind.

It was a clear, sunny, blue sky morning when we hit Buckingham Palace, where we enjoyed another photo shoot outside. It was eerily quiet, and there was hardly anyone around. In fact, no one, save us four. And so we claimed the Palace as the new site for the Outer Limits Comic Shop! Viva la Revolution, baby!

We all needed to see to our ablutions, and so we checked into the Hyde Park Toilet facility so that we could shave, brush our teeth, wash behind our ears, things like that. However, a loud moaning in a cubicle disturbed our hygiene routine. In the mirror, Paul glanced at me sideways while I was washing my face with a flannel. Our eyes met. We turned in unison to the sound. The moaning turned into wailing, in what we could discern to most likely be Russian.

"Nieeeetttttt!"

Some crazy Russian guy with a scar running along his face banged out of the cubicle with clenched fists and smacked his head against the mirror besides us. He was half-naked, and yet again he moaned and cursed. If that wasn't enough, he continued to repeatedly bang his head against the mirror! (Remember my reference to our ever-expanding portfolio of weirdos?)

"Time to go, Jay," Paul whispered, dragging me away by my coat sleeve. "This isn't our problem." And he was right.

Camden Market. All I have to say to that is "Wow!" to quote a Jedi Master, while removing his hood Kenobi style.

Paul intoned, "I have never seen a more wretched hive of scum and villainy. We must be cautious."

As we moved into the bizarre market, we all heard and then spotted a pure black Volkswagen beetle, a post-war model. It was highly polished and, on the bonnet, air-brushed by some brilliant artist, I might add, was an infamous Brian Bolland "Killing Joke" from Batman. *[Jay Note: The Killing Joke was a classic graphic novel by Alan Moore and the aforementioned artist, Brian Bolland.]* Some clown was actually driving it slowly through the market! The cool bastard! The windows were blacked-out; it was utterly incredible.

"Holy fornicate, Batman!" was Paul's awed comment. Surely this was a good omen? A sign from the comic gods themselves? A way for them to bless us on our crusade!

Moving through the stalls we saw some weird stuff. Some Monk dude with a shaved head wearing an orange robe and carrying a two-by-four over his head passed us by. A guy in a crate — yes, crate — playing Jimmy Hendrix on a wah-wah pedal and some young girl with dirty mousy hair said to Robert,

"Do you want to buy a flower?" before bumping into him. Luckily, Robert was savvy and held her hands as she tried to pickpocket him.

"Not today, honey. Go home, run to Fagin, love."

It was an eye-opener for us — me, especially.

Further on in our voyage through the market, I saw a woman in her early thirties crying uncontrollably, and my heart went out to her. All this reminded me of that song, "Streets of London", by Ralph McTell.

"Have you seen the old man

in the closed-down market

kicking up the paper,

with his worn-out shoes?

In his eyes you'll see no pride,

hands held loosely by his side.

Yesterday's paper telling yesterday's news.

So how can you tell me,

you're lonely,

And say for you that the sun doesn't shine?

Let me take you by the hand and I'll lead you through the streets of London,

I'll show you something that'll make you change your mind."

We asked in the local hostel where Mega City, the comic shop, was and an unshaved homeless guy kindly informed us. We thanked him.

And so, soon enough, we were almost at our journey's end. Some crowds were gathered there already, and so we decided to muscle-in and browse round the so-called Mega City.

Paul and Robert introduced themselves to the owners. They were virgins in every sense of the word. Too much *Black Kiss* and *Faust* comics, I reckon.

Paul said, "We run a comic shop in Lisburn, Northern Ireland, and we met Pat Mills in Belfast."

"Oh, I see," replied the owner, coldly and zombie-like. "There is a bit of dust on the window I must apply my intention to," he continued with his monosyllabic tone of voice. He shuffled off.

Paul was taken aback and slapped his sides, dusting them down. He turned to me wide-eyed and called the shopkeeper a familiar word rhyming with "banker."

"Don't worry, Paul matey," I assured my comrade. "I am sure Pat will recognise me!"

Soon, more crowds arrived and we jostled for position. Eventually, I heard Pat's voice and, finally, through the crowds, I saw him and Simon Bisley. They were discussing *Slaine's* artwork as they sat down. Good thing, too. If they'd been standing, they surely would have had heart failure with the amount of fan-boy explosion and adulation they were about to encounter! I knew all of us there would treat them like movie stars, like on an apocalyptic scale!

My mouth was dry with excitement. I stood upright with my hands on my hips, my head back and said with my best Ulster accent,

"Hello, Pat! Do you remember me?"

Simultaneously, Robert unleashed his flashing telescopic camera!

The crowds ducked for cover, as did the owners of the enemy shop, but when they discovered they weren't under a terrorist attack (yet), they decided to relax.

I shook Pat's hand and he laughed out loud when recognition dawned!

"Angela," he turned to a lady, with dark curly hair and holding a handbag, standing next to him. "This is the guy from Belfast I was talking about! The heckler!" He twisted his seat towards Simon. "This guy!" He couldn't believe his eyes.

We all burst into laughter when he said that.

"So what brings you guys here? Do I really need to ask?"

When he saw the huge amount of graphic novels, progs, annuals, albums and *Marshal Laws* for him and Simon to inscribe their monikers on, I'm sure he fancied doing a runner. But, with his good nature, the party continued.

"We came all the way from Northern Ireland just to see you, Pat!" I said. "It's been a real adventure! So is this the Angie Mills?" I was turning on the old Irish charm, shaking the lady's hand gallantly, although I don't think the others were paying her much attention.

"I have something here for you to sign. Pat signed last time I met him and, well, it would be my honour if you could sign this for me?" I handed over the first appearance of Slaine in *2000 AD*.

The guys were busy talking to Simon while Robert continued snapping. Alan and Paul remarked that Simon looked uncannily like Paul. They both wore woolly jumpers and glasses and had the same long hairstyle!

I continued to chat away to Pat.

"Pat, I'm sorry if I gave you a rough time in Belfast with the *Crisis* rubbish — but we all love *Slaine*! You should know that! But a bit less of the Earth Mother nonsense! It's all getting a bit too namby- pamby!" I winced.

Paul agreed. "Oh come on, Pat, give us blood! Give us what we want! There's not enough blood and guts! We're all Celts!"

We all roared in unison, like a tribal chant,

"We are Celts and want more blood!"

The looks on Pat's and Simon's faces were a picture. There was a mixture of shock and amazement. They were utterly flabbergasted!

We realised soon enough, however, that time was precious. Some very talented young artists were vying for the attention of the Horned Gods. Eventually, Alan got Simon's phone number and we said farewell to Pat, Angela and Simon.

Pat said, "Good luck, Celts, and safe home to Northern Ireland!"

"Okay, Pat, and fare ye well!" was my reply.

We all turned away. I turned back but he was too busy signing to pay us any more attention. I guess that is what is known as "show business." The show must go on.

After the excitement and drama, we were tired, exhausted, more like it, but we found time to consume a croissant. My first ever! And each of us grabbed a foot-long hot dog from a pastry shop beside the Mega City. And there, outside, with our mouths full of mustard, ketchup, buns and sausage, we saw through the assembled masses no other than Cat Weasel!

"Hey, gang!" He announced cheerfully! "It's been done."

And it was.

We headed home on the Oxford Street tube and that was when I saw her. During a time when my mind couldn't have been further away from the fairer sex! She had long, curly blonde hair, and red-pouting lips turned up into a knowing smile. She was the Earth Goddess.

154

"*Sometimes I am your Mother and I hold you, sometimes I am your sister and I befriend you…and other times, I am your lover and I stick a knife in your back…*"

She looked at me, just once, mind you, but then she left at the next stop. Nevertheless, that beauty was the absolute pinnacle to the best weekend of my life. "Now, onwards to the next mighty, heroic adventure!" *[Jay Note: quotation Pat Mills.]*

In Mega City
Left to right: Jonathan, Pat Mills and Angie

CHAPTER FOURTEEN: CLASH OF THE TITANS - PART TWO

It was The Clash of the Titans. It was Achilles vs. Hector; Saddam Hussein vs. George Bush Senior; The Silver Surfer vs. Galacticus; it was Gilgamesh vs. that other guy! It was Judge Dredd, a.k.a. me vs. the flying fists of Stan Lee, a.k.a Richard the Munnisher Munn.

And what were the stakes, I hear you ask? Why, the honour of the Outer Limits Comic Shop, of course! And, perhaps most importantly, a conclusion had been drawn to the long-debated question: who is the best comic character of all time?

Round One! *Fight!*

Ah, I remember it well! We were all milling round the shelves of our friendly neighbourhood comic shop. Paul was sitting playing his electric guitar at the helm whilst looking out the shop window, as he usually did. Gary, the elder brother, was sitting on the stool facing him, cross-legged, reading Fangoria magazine. The Munnisher was reading *The Punisher* comic, leaning on the shelf where *Marvel* hid its shame and I was perusing *The Tick* comic on the opposite shelf. We were all waiting for something or someone…

We heard a soft step coming from upstairs. Paul stopped strumming his guitar. Gary paused from rustling through his magazine, looking upwards. A dog barked outside the window, and the traffic seemed to slow outside. A flake of dust hung in the still air, glistening in the sunlight. There was a breathless whisper, like an intake of air when someone sighs. Richard wiped the sweat from his forehead.

No one spoke.

There was the sound of chains being unlocked.

And a lovely old lady, with glasses perched at the tip of her nose, appeared at the door. With a tray in her hands, she came bearing proper tea and biscuits. It was Mrs M! I feel it only proper to introduce the Mother of the Malones in an official capacity. She is, after all, the saintly old dear who not only brought us tea, but also brought the Malones into this world as well.

From upstairs we had the most amazing parties. One extreme party resulted in the family cat's litter tray being used as a bed for Gavin Curly Hughes during his drunken coma. He got paralytic with vodka and I saved him from choking to death on his own vomit (and cat litter) in the upstairs bathroom. His parents grounded him for a year afterwards.

"Oh, hi, Mrs M! Let me take that tray from you!" I said with a smile.

"That's okay, Jay, I can manage!" replied the feisty Ann.

"Paul," she scolded her son. "Clear a space, and put your guitar away."

Paul rolled his eyes.

"Thanks, Mum," Gary said.

Max appeared on the stairs mewing at the Munnisher, purring around Mama Malone's feet. Because of the kettle incident, we all decided it was best for all concerned to have Mrs M do the tea from now on.

"Enjoy your tea boys!" she said as

Mrs Malone

she pottered upstairs again. "Come on Max." She shooed her pussy upstairs with her. Max was aptly named for his gargantuan proportion. He was the size and build of a canine. Not a small dog, but the size of a medium sized one. When we first saw him we thought they were feeding Max Godzilla cat food. Maxilla pounded up the stairs.

Paul Malone and Max the cat

We all had our tea and biscuits — custard creams which we dunked and allowed to melt in our mouths. Beautiful. Fully recharged, the Munnisher and myself got into yet another debate about Judge Dredd and the Punisher…

"Yeah, yeah, Johnny," Rick sneered. "What about the time when Judge Dredd was beat to a pulp by — who was it, now?" He paused to think. "Oh! Stan Lee, the greatest martial artist to emerge from the nuclear radiation of the Atomic Wars in China! Now he kicked his ass!" Rick guffawed, leering into my face.

"That's true, Munn," I grimly said, my jaw set. "However, at their next encounter, it was a completely different story."

"I don't believe you, Fisher!" he spat.

"Oh, don't you? Don't you? Do you? Well…" I pounced like a coiled panther to the back of the shop, tearing my way through the back issues of *2000 AD*. Finally, I found my quarry, smacking the two relative progs on the counter, seeking the encounter between Deathfist, Stan Lee and the Judge.

"There, Munn!"

As if by some celestial transformer device, the mighty Power Cosmic, the Munnisher and I were transformed into the almighty Judge and Stan Lee. The battle was joined!

"Ha! I spit on your justice system, Dredd! I defeated you once!" His fist became a flurry of blows to the Judge's body. "I can succeed again! On three-D vision this time, as well — complete with an audience, Dredd!" He laughed manically.

The Judge struck a blow to his jaw, but he knew his style now and he wasn't going to let Stan Lee win. Reeling from this first attack, the Deathfist knew this wasn't going to be easy. He counteracted with a spinning dropkick.

There was a whirl of strokes and parries and, eventually, the Judge backed off slightly, wanting to regroup. Up a stairwell they fought, battling every inch of the way. Ferociously, they battled. Raw-fisted Stan Lee was bleeding slightly from the Judge's onslaught.

Thawk! Grunt! Kapow!

Judge Dredd was feeling it, but he refused to give in this time.

With a maddened roar, Stan Lee was going berserk with fury. A fatal mistake. The Judge's training — fifteen years in the Academy of Law— meant he was an expert in all forms of combat. His combatant, on the other hand, was a disciple of the martial arts school in the radiation lands of Ji. Quite simply, no contest.

They fought through a Mall, like a maelstrom. The shoppers screamed and headed for cover as the two duellists came to blows. All this time, a camera crew was filming the action and it was being broadcast all over Mega-City One.

"Folks at home! Do not touch that dial! This is live action at its best!"

Judge Dredd finally found his advantage. The Deathfist was angry and, with all his might, he launched into a final onslaught. But the Judge honed in for the kill, knocking the so-called Deathfist out cold with a seemingly easy uppercut to the chin. Stan Lee just stood for a brief moment and crumpled over onto the slab.

"Yes!" I laughed victoriously.

"Report, Judge Dredd," said Chief Judge Silver in his baritone voice. "Why didn't you just use your Lawgiver to bring him to Justice?"

"Yes, Chief Justice." The Judge's voice was deep, and reverberated around the Grand Hall of Justice. He continued,

"I decided it was better to bring the perpetrator to justice by fisticuffs to show

160

the citizens that justice may bend."

Now, I was returning to reality from the cosmic fugue.

"But never ever break!" I was shouting, purple with rage.

Paul and Gary were in fits of laughter, while the Munnisher looked crestfallen. He didn't say a word.

"Oh, Jay," Paul said. "You missed a frame!"

Chief Judge Silver paused, looked over his shoulder when he was leaving on his walking stick, and said to the Judge with a wink,

"Oh and Dredd? *Damn good fight!*"

Gary Malone with Max

The Astrozombies
Left to right: Keith Møller, Derek Lockhart, Richard Munn, Peter Blake (comicshopian) and Jonathan

Chapter Fifteen: The Party That Never Ended

My twenty-first birthday party was a day like no other.

There are events in people's lives that explode into others, almost like a chain reaction. A bit like Tolkien, it was long expected and long since planned for.

People refer to legends as an act, a story which is spread by nothing more than simple, pre-technology word of mouth and gossip, passed down from generation to generation. This day was a legend in its truest form. This was my finest hour. And my fellow band members, to give them their credit, were Richard Munn, Derek Lockhart and Keith Møller.

"We are the Astrozombies, and we are one, one thirty-eight in the eye of the tigggggggeeeeeeerrrrrrrrrrrr!" (This song is based on the character *THX 1138*, George Lucas's first science fiction movie, cosmic fact, fans.)

Prior to all this, we practised our dark arts at the old Orange Hall on Railway Street. Derek, I believe, was a lodge member, and walked on July twelfth, like his father before him, and his forefathers, etc. Anyway, he was the drummer of our band, and he could drum the devil out of his very Hell. Next was Keith, brother of Marty, the Scandinavians who frequented the Outer Limits comic shop. Keith could play the base guitar with real attitude. Then cometh the hour, cometh the axe man: Richard Munn. In his prime, with his mane of the curliest of hair, he was no doubt the best guitar player this side of the great divide.

The band perfected their art in the Hall of Orange.

We were ready.

Then there was me: Jonathan Fisher, son of Emma and William, twin of David. I painted my face in the guise of Lobo, the comic character developed by Alan Grant and Simon Bisley. The character himself had a beard and two large black wings covering his eyes, and said the words "Frag off" and "son of a bastich", instead of the usual profanity swear words. Marty Møller had kindly lent me his Misfits "skull" teeshirt — the wardrobe and image were complete!

We were the ultimate Misfits tribute band, and then some!

Keith and Rick had teeshirts to suit the occasion. The Munnisher wore his "Slayer" teeshirt beneath his mighty mane. Keith himself had an "evil never dies" teeshirt. Derek, on the other hand, never needed a teeshirt. He simply put on an ordinary thing. After all, his drumming spoke for itself.

I had, err, "liberated" Bryson House's photocopier machine for my own purposes, the results comprising one four-foot large Danzig skull which myself and Keith and a few others positioned above the drum kit and Richard's awesome Marshal amplifier.

I had everyone at my party: friends, friends of friends, friends of friends of friends. It was going to be one hell of an evening — and I'd make sure of that. My own dear mother had forewarned the neighbourhood of a possible apocalyptical event.

"And it most certainly was, Stanley." *[Jay Note: reference to Laurel and Hardy.]*

The crowd had gathered en masse, all in the back garden. People laughed, and beer, spirits and tobacco were consumed by the gallon.

We started the set list, "Tweeeeeeeeennnnntttttttlllyyyyy eyes in my head, they're all the same!" Then we continued with Astrozombies' "With just a touch of my burning hand…" I made sure I did all the actions, waving my left hand across the garden, then turning it into a fist.

"I send my Astrozombies to rape this land (accompanied with a few groin thrusts!). Prime directive: exterminate the whole human race, your face drops in a pile of flesh and your heart pumps till it pumps in death! Prime directive: exterminate this fraggin' place! All I wanted to say — and all I wanna do — is, who do I do this for? Hey me or you?!"

The crowd met our entertainment with great applause and this was only the entourage!

Tada dum, dummmm! went Keith's bass and Rick's guitar. The air began to melt between the amps. And we all shouted in unison,

"Martian!"

"Oh go! Possession of the mind is a terrible thing! It's a transformation with an urge to kill! Not the body of a man from earth, not the face of the one you love. Well, I turned into a Martian!"

Then, to my horror, I realised something: all these legendary golden songs weren't being recorded! They had been lost to the very mists of time and space. Only to witnesses will they live forever.

Fortunately, however, I had pressed the record button on my trustee "sing along system", which comprised no more than a basic tape deck. But the rest, as they say, is history.

"Where eagles dare…" And we did.

"Mommy can I go out and…" Every band member roared in unison:

"*Kill tonight.*"

"Night of the living dead…" Awesome drum roll from the seventh-level drummer.

"Ghouls night out…" Richard the Munnisher heartily enthused, "This is what this party's all about — this is a ghouls' night out!"

"Hallowe'en! Freddy! Marty!" I called to my legion. "Do you remember Hallowe'en?

"Some kinda hate… the slow song, for all you lovers of rock out there, '*Bullet*.'"

Right on target.

And then some.

Jonathan, aged 19. Self-portrait

Deep in the spider's web, the spider was going insane… Slowly, and execrably he began his plans against me… but this was my day, the day like no other. His malice-filled mind was full of hate against me. He had evil schemes, twisted fitful dreams…

When the sun was setting, the legion intuitively and instinctively joined me in the kitchen like bats coming in to roost. Picture it. It was incredible. We joined in like a tribal instinct. I swear I had an orgasm with the last few songs! The crowd roared in unison to "Long way back from Hell"… "Snakes of Christ"… "Twist of Cain"… "Hallowe'en reprise"…

And then it was over.

Food was served. Some select alumni were invited to the living room where we played a Danzig video. Friends agreed that this video, although cool by Glenn's high standard, wasn't as good as the monster rock-fest I and my fellow Zombies had put on there in the back garden!

We all chatted till around half eleven. Eventually, the guests left and I hugged them all individually in the front garden. The air was still, and a full moon hung in the summer air. All guests, save one, went home that evening: Richard Munn.

He wanted to stay behind in the living room. I knew his reasons for wanting to stay. I hugged him very hard, and went upstairs with a very drunk Dona, my new girlfriend.

What Richard thought that evening he never fully said. He said it was so quiet that night he could even hear a spider spinning its web in the corner…

166

you are cordially invited to
THE
JOHN FISHER
WORLD - DOMINATION
MEGA - APOCALYPTIC
21st BIRTHDAY
B L I T Z K R E I G
to be held at
38 RATHVARNA GARDENS, LISBURN
on the 26th July 1991
FEATURING THE
ASTROZOMBIES
and you'd better believe it !

'Let the gashing start! Vigourously I want the crimson fluid to flow! Loud I like the wailing and not without cause! For...corpses headless and limp...bodies with no surprises...these are pleasing words to me...'

'KISS MY AXE !'

'by the end of the night they're gonna be mindf--ked !'
- Rick Munn -Lead Guitarist and Astrozombie

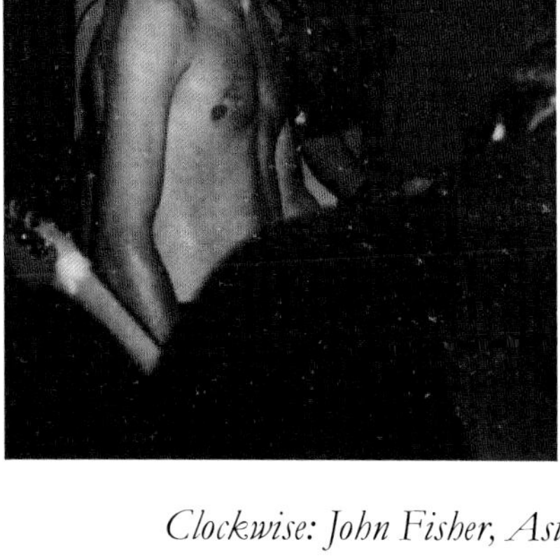

Clockwise: John Fisher, Astrozombie. Jonathan and Dona. Jonathan. Richard Munn, Gary Hughes and Jonathan. Jonathan, Alan and Stewart Reid

168

Thud the Barbarian, by Jonathan, aged 19

CHAPTER SIXTEEN: THAT RAINY DAY

It was a rainy day in Lisburn town, like it seems to rain every day in Lisburn. It has a seemingly intentional habit of doing it on purpose. Damn you, Atlantic Ocean and jet stream! Damn you to Hell!

I was on foot, en route to Outer Limits, the friendly neighbourhood comic shop. I decided to wear my dad's green fishing coat and my Australian hat which Mum had brought home for me when she went to see her uncle Jack from the land from down under. Huddled beneath it, crouched with the collar up, my disguise was complete. My feet were soaking through my gutties, though. Damn the rain!

Anyway, I passed by the window down Bridge Street to see who was in the shop. Paul and Heather were all cosy and warm with the wee fan heater blowing as they sat beside each other.

I opened the door.

Menacingly, I closed it shut. Head down, so my friends couldn't recognise me, I went straight to the back of the shop where my rampage was set to begin.

They began to whisper. Paul said to Heather,

"Who the hell is this guy?"

I started to moan, lowly.

"Filth. *Marvel* filth." I pulled the comics off the shelves and onto the floor. "Flith! Pure flith!" I muffled more loudly.

"Marvel Filth, Marvel Filth, it's just a load of Marvel Filth,

It's got no plot, it's just trash — a waste of time and your cash!

Hey man! Stan Lee spawns his Marvel Filth, Marvel Filth!

Marvel Filth, Marvel Filth! It's just a load of Marvel Filth,

Wolverine he is quite obscene — deserves his seat on toilet scene!

As for The Hulk — he just makes me sulk,

The Fantastic Four makes me sore — it's such a bore and a chore!

Watch out! Because it's Marvel Filth!

Because it's just a load of Marvel Filth!

Hey man! Stan Lee spawns his Marvel Filth!"

(Sung to the tune of the cartoon classic, Spider-man!)

"Oh, hi, Jay!" Heather laughed aloud.

I paused my maelstrom for a second and then pulled off my hat and shook it fiercely. I laughed and turned to face them. I grinned and sat down on the stool facing them.

"How did you recognise me, Heather? Was it your female intuition? Your female instinct? Your sixth sense? What blew it?"

Heather added with a smirk, "It was your shoes, Jay! We recognised your gutties!" She lay back against the wall, her stool perched at an angle.

Paul laughed when recognition dawned.

"You want a towel, Jay? There's one out the back."

"Thanks, Paul," I said when he handed me the towel. I dried my ears first, shaking them like a dog. "Brrrrr! It's kind of wet out there!"

I stood up and picked up the comics from the floor before gingerly putting them on the shelf.

"Why can't *Marvel* comics produce a comic called Water Guy? Oh…" I paused, looking down, shaking my head in disgust.

"There is Aquamandude. Could I see what's in my bag, Paul matey?"

"Sure, Jay," replied Paul, his glasses full of steam. He took them off and wiped them with a tissue from his mighty pocket.

The "bags" were a term we used for unsold comics, which the Malones were kind enough to let us buy when we had the money. They had the bags in order. One such bag belonged to a guy called Fergal John Whiteman. I gave him the name of Fergal because he looked a bit like Fergal Sharkey. Anyway, this train wreck of a guy went to Wallace High School and was a friend of Stewart Reido, who looked a bit like Paul Atreides from my favourite film *Dune*. So I got Paul's big black marker and started writing on Fergal's bag.

It had started innocently enough, but his comics were appalling — all porno comics! I guess he simply had to be punished by his peers.

And I was the one who started it.

Obviously, Richard the Munnisher enthusiastically joined in. We started writing "John Fergal, Faust-loving, fornicating, Friesian cow fondling, fatuous, fartmeister, festering, franked, frumpily flambéed, face ache, frankenfurter" — and many other insults that we could think of culminating with "fallopian fingering." This had to be done, dear reader, you must understand.

A few weeks later, John Whiteman featured on The John Fisher Radio show. Wow! In my exposé of *The Faust* comic, this was filth. This had to be done for the sake of children everywhere — and civilisation, as we know it.

We recorded some samples from *Blackadder II*, with the infamous baby-eating bishop of Bath and Wells helping us. The report went something like this.

"Hello! Good evening, citizens, and welcome to the Fisher report," I began in an official tone. In the background, the sound of papers rustling could be heard, almost like that of a news-reporter on the television.

"Tonight, we have shocking news of a corrupt individual and even of a corrupt comic. Or should that be the other way round? Anyway, this person is addicted to a comic."

And then the bishop joins in at this point.

"I am a colossal pervert — John Whiteman." (Marty Møller voice-over, instead of Blackadder). "No form of sexual gratification is too low for me: animal, vegetable or mineral. I would do anything to anything!" the bishop rumbled.

I continued the investigation. "Our investigation continues," I said soberly. "Our trail leads us to Mrs Whiteman, mother of Fergal, the home residence of I-am-a-colossal-pervert John Whiteman. No form of sexual gratifications is too low for me: animal, vegetable or mineral. I would do anything to anything!"

I pressed for an interview with Mrs Whiteman. There was a knock on the door (Marty obliged with the sound effects, knocking on the bedroom door).

"Mrs Whiteman, Mrs Whiteman, let us in, Mrs Whiteman. This is The John Fisher Radio show somewhere in the Lisburn area, broadcasting to you on one-o-eight megahertz, listen or die. We want to interview you!"

No answer.

There was a sound of muffled sniggering from Marty and Alan.

At this point, I decided I would play the part of Mrs Whiteman.

"Who is it?" I said in high-pitched, squeaky, trying-to-be-feminine voice.

And then, "Let us in, you fat bitch!"

Marty pulled his cabinet and bookcase to one side for effect.

And we were in!

I solemnly interviewed Mrs Whiteman.

"So, Mrs Whiteman, we meet at last! What have you to say for yourself?"

She continued. "I am a colossal pervert — John Whiteman. No form of sexual gratification is too low for me: animal, vegetable or mineral. I would do anything to anything!"

"But surely, Mrs Whiteman, this is not the case?" I further enquired. "Our inquiries find you blameless. Is this not the case?"

"Oh, it's twue, it's twue," she sobbed, suddenly developing a lisp. "My poor John was cowwupted by those wowwable boys at that shop. Outer Limits? Yeah, that's the one."

"Indeed, Mrs Whiteman. Do continue," I insisted. "I am here for you. I share your pain because Outer Limits doesn't have a regular supply of comics. Damn the distributors. They forced the store to stock inferior comics rather than *2000 AD* — the Galaxy's greatest comic. Now they're forced to stock crappy *Marvel* and *DC comics*. And, of course, *Faust, Black Kiss* and some French pervy porn comics. Other lovers of this filth include Rick Munn, Alan McColonicIrrigation, Gary Malone, Robert Malone, Paul Malone, and Paul Andrews. The list goes on!"

"Yo!" I added my trademark at the end.

"Do you have any last words, Mrs Whiteman?"

"I am a colossal pervert — John Whiteman. No form of sexual gratification is too low for me: animal, vegetable or mineral. I would do anything to anything!"

So it was decided that Fergal would listen to it in the comic shop. It was only fair, I suppose. He was, err, invited by his school chums, let's say. Okay, that's a bit of a lie. All his form persuaded him. Okay, that's not strictly true either. They all dragged him to his execution — and that is true.

Well, our "interview" was being broadcast simultaneously by our "contact", who will, dear reader, remain nameless.

We were all assembled at the shop. The whole of Fergal's form was there, including Reido, Marty, Alan, Richard Munn, Paddy and Rick Black.

"Listen up, everyone!" I called out, standing on a stool. "Order! Order!"

"Feck off, Fisher!" someone retorted.

My eyes narrowed, searching for the heckler. The comic shop was full. All the juves were jostling about. I couldn't find him but, by the holy jockstrap of Robert E. Howard, he'd pay for that hell-spawn!

Anyway, I announced tonight's main attraction.

"Tonight, the main attraction, my friends, will be submitted for your approval." I paused, building the tension.

"There will be a special edition of the John Fisher Radio show, exposé of *Faust* comic! Paul, if you would be so kind to tune in the frequency?" I sat down from the stool.

Paul obliged and put in a cassette to record the special radio blitzkrieg.

After the music faded, I was introduced by Marty. I could see the look on Fergal's face. He was inwardly squirming, fidgeting his feet.

When Fergal heard his name mentioned, his eyes bulged out of their sockets and lunged toward the tape deck. It was like slow motion! He leapt at Paul's cassette recorder like a salmon, but it seemed that the whole shop dived at him like a huge rugby scrum, pulling him back!

"No!" he wailed.

How were we to know that his Mum, according to all reports, as Marty and Richard Munn told us, was an overweight lady and a female dog?

We broke Fergal's mind that day, the poor guy. Justice was done — Just-us!

Meanwhile, back on that rainy day, my comic bag contained *The Last American*, *Toxic!*, *Alien Legion*, and *The Tick* — all good comics in their day, let me tell you. I purchased them with my galactic groats. I settled back to read them on the stool.

Heather left us to go to her photography class in Belfast, after the obligatory smooch from her boyfriend, that is. She took her leave with her umbrella, which was out the back. I sat beside my best friend, Paul Malone.

When Marty Møller decided to remake *Dune* in the comic shop, he and I acted out some scenes from it. He loved the 1994 David Lynch version just as much as I did.

"What do you call the mouse shadow on the second moon?" I would say to Marty.

He would reply, with his sniggering laugh,

"We call that one Ma'lone!"

"So may I be known as Paul Ma'lone?"

Marty never kept a straight face. He laughed.

"You are Paul Ma'lone, and we welcome you to our tribe!"

Stewart Reid

We were all characters from *Dune*: Frederick Faustenegger was Feyd-Rautha, and Stewart Reido was Paul Atreides, Paul Andrews the Baron Harkonnen! Stewart relished the role, shouting "Muad'Dib!" at the top of his voice.

I considered myself a bit of a Duncan Idaho.

One time, in the past, I recall the time Aynat cruelly dumped Paul for Alan McColonicIrrigation. Paul was devastated but soon found solace in the arms of Heather H. I was furious with the two As. How could they do that to their friend and lover?

So a plot was formed in my mind. How do you get back at such a treachery? How do you insult two arse-holes? I found a way. *I always do.*

It happened on the way back from the Coach in Banbridge. Marty Møller, Rick Black, Paddy, Paul and myself all squeezed ourselves into Rick Black's taxi, while Alan, Aynat and Heather H went in Alan's car. We all went out that night for a bit of boogying, but it ended up like a rave in a shit-hole.

Still incensed by Alan's behaviour, and sitting in the front seat, I told Rick to get beside them.

"Rick, get alongside Alan's car."

He was doing seventy miles an hour. Rick thought I was going to give them the finger, but this was not quite the case. Paul was in the back seat close to tears, but he was bearing up. A good man and a good friend.

I wound down the automatic window. I pulled at my belt, and pulled down my breaks.

I shoved my ass out of Richard Black's car window at seventy miles an hour, and waved in the direction of the enemy car.

"Jay? What the fuck are you doing?" exclaimed Rick.

But Paul was in fits of laughter, as were the rest of the guys.

Job done, I thought.

Alan was in shock, but Aynat, the perv, clearly quite liked it. She threw back her head and roared with laughter. Ah well, you can't win them all.

Paul and I sat for hours on end, sometimes playing chess. Sometimes he tried to teach me some guitar chords, and sometimes we would get a delivery from the distributors. It was like gold from El Dorado! Those days were sporadic at best, despite Paul's order book, which plotted out the week's orders in advance. We even had teeshirts! At last, we were a comic shop!

I bought a "Marshal Law — Nuke me slowly." A few other guys bought teeshirts with other comic characters and symbols emblazoned on them.

I asked Paul, "Paul, matey, who in their right fraggin' mind bought this travesty? It's awful! Crap! Balls! Rubbish!" I held it up and read it aloud in a monosyllabic tone of voice.

"I am Nemesis. I am the Death Bringer."

Paul Andrews sheepishly held his hand up.

"It's me. I bought it. What'sth wrong with it, Johnny? Even Glenn Danzigth wore it in his video!" He swiped it like a hawk, or rather a vulture, from my grasp.

This was true. The evil Elvis Glenn Danzig himself wore it in one of his videos.

"Okay, Paul, you may live to spawn. Go forth and proclaim that Outer Limits is a comic shop. Yeah!"

With the Tits-up suppliers, we got a lot of publicity material. I decided to go forth, like Andrews, to put posters on cars, Ulsterbuses, prams, bicycles, dogs — anything that would move, really, with the aim of spreading the word.

I managed to put a lot on Ulsterbuses that moved down Bridge Street.

"Hold still, damn you!" I said to one bus.

"Here, doggie!" I said to a dog, bribing it with a Marathon bar.

There was this one time I saw a child's pram, complete with child. I was just passing by Wicked Wendy's Soft Furnishings, and the child's mother went in and left the baby in the pram, with the brake off, no less! Jay to the rescue! Like the six-million-dollar dude, I bounded to put the brake on. To quote Spider dude, "Action is my only reward." And, of course, a poster for the kid in the pram.

They were the good days in the comic shop. Halcyon days. Damn good days.

At the time, *Twin Peaks* was on BBC 2 and we all came in one day and started quoting from it.

"Mmmm, that's a damn fine cup of coffee!" we would say.

"That's damn fine blueberry pie!"

The Munnisher worked in Greanz Food Emporium where we got supplies — the usual suspects: doughnuts and cherry pie — for our consumption and devouring. Damn fine.

One day, Paul I and were sitting when this biker dude, complete with Viking beard, sun glasses, and a massive Harley Davidson, parked his hog right outside the shop door.

"Holy fuck!" was Paul's comment as he stood up and peaked out of the window.

The guy bounded into the shop, removed his glasses, put them into his denim jacket pocket, took off his helmet and said,

"Holy fuck, boys, it's a comic shop!" He looked around for a second, and then added, "In holy fucking Lisburn!"

He shook our hands.

"Dave Graham's the name! Holy fucking God!" He browsed around for a while, taking note of the Independent comics.

While Paul chatted to Dave about his hog, I found out that he was a massive *2000 AD* fan. He loved "Invasion 1999" in the progs.

"Oh, yeah! Bill Savage is the man! You remember that episode with Bill Savage in the bath, smoking a stogie — a cigar, that is — playing with his rubber ducky, and he has his big fuckin' shot gun in the bath with him? And remember when the Volgans burst in? He blasts the holy fucking crap out of them with his shotgun, saying 'Quack! Quack! Volg!'"

"What a pure classic that line is!" I agreed with him, laughing. "Pat Mills is a genius!"

Despite the cheerful, entertaining and otherwise fantastic people who would frequent the comic shop, other less than salubrious characters with bad hygiene disorders would visit on occasion. One such person was simply named, "The Bag Man." This poor guy wandered the streets of Lisburn searching for the one thing that made his life meaningful: plastic shopping bags of every description. He collected them and put them in a holdall. Bags within bags; bags within other bags. The poor wretch had a duffle coat and a hat — a floppy rain hat, no less. Some say he was a tutor at Lisburn Tech who lost the plot. Others speak various other mumblings, like how he was a genius but had cracked up. Other people veered away from his past and focused more on his present, stating that he, quite simply, stank to high heaven. But he did, of course. I remember, on one occasion, I tried to have a conversation with the guy while trying not to bring my pie back up, and Paul stood covering his mouth with his jumper. I wish I could say we had an intellectual conversation, and how I realised you really shouldn't judge a book by its cover, but the guy talked like a crazy lunatic. Enough said.

One night, the guys and myself were upstairs in the Malones' flat above the comic shop, relaxing after a day's work. There was Mrs M, who was curled up on her favourite chair with her pussycat Max, Paul and Heather were on the sofa bed, along with the effeminate Frederick Faustenegger, who was totally flirting with Heather and Paul. I was sitting beside Robert on the two-seater beside the window. My eyes narrowed at Faustenegger, he was such a lady-killer. I was jealous of this guy, as he was a mean guitarist and a meaner chess player who beat me hands down. But Frederick was a great guy, and a very loveable rogue. Bit like me.

Anyway, the gigolo said, "Outer Limits is like *Cheers*, isn't it?" He wiped his dirty fair hair away from his face, crossed his legs and produced a cigarette from a packet secreted from his back pocket.

"Don't worry, Johnny, I'll take it downstairs to light it," he added, mumbling with it in his mouth. He stepped over Paul and Heather. Maxi-pussy mewed at him in passing.

We all loved *Cheers* and, true enough, every Friday night, Channel 4, we were there, whether upstairs in the shop eating pizzas, having parties, or playing Space Crusade, Risk, and Shogun. Great times.

"Making your way in the world today takes everything you've got. Taking a break from all your worries, sure would help a lot. Wouldn't you like to get away…?" We would sing over the theme tune. *"…To Outer Limits comic shop! Where everybody knows your name, and they're always glad you came!"*

This particular Friday evening it was getting late and we heard a noise coming from across the road. I looked out the window and across the street, looking downwards and towards The Olde Castilian Bar and Grill. Simultaneously, Frederick ran up the stairs and said out of breath,

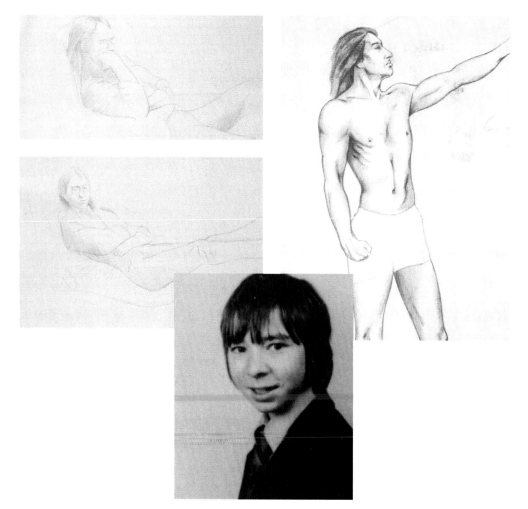

Various ages of Paul Malone. Sketches drawn by Jonathan

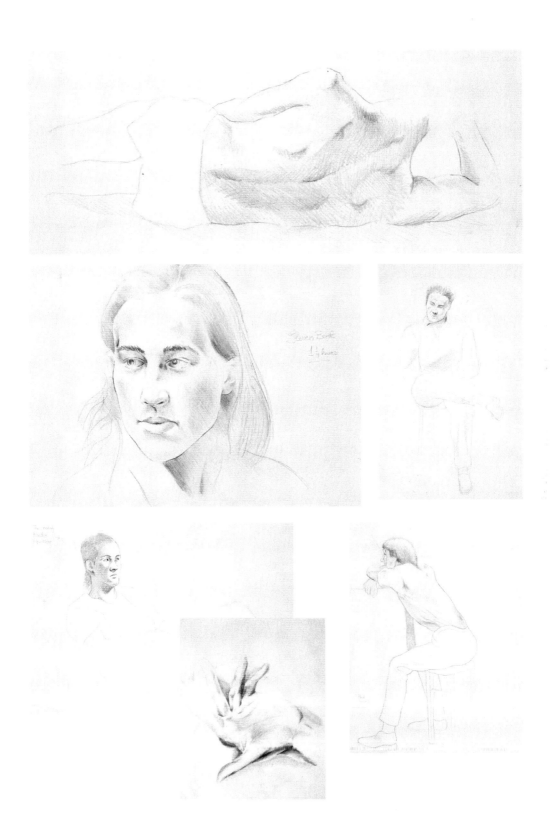

181

Clockwise: Paul's back. Alan Nicholl. Stewart Reid. Jonathan's hand.
Heather Hamilton. Stephen Bent. Drawn by Jonathan

"Holy feck! Turn the lights off quick!"

On the television, Arnie was battling against *The Predator*, but it was nothing compared to what we witnessed that night!

I knew it was going to be a war zone. A full fraggin' scale riot was to ensue in Bridge Street.

We all stood up looking out onto the street below us. There were police Land Rovers, at least fifteen of them parked outside, up the street, surrounding the inn. There were two army wagons there as well. There were officers in full riot gear and police dogs disgorged from the back of the Land Rovers, snarling viciously.

"Cry 'Havoc!' and let slip the dogs of war!"

Maxi-pussy squirmed out of Mrs M's arms quick as he could make it, straight to the upstairs toilet where his cat litter tray was waiting. That cat was lightning fast for his considerable bulk!

What we gathered was that some off-duty squaddies had enjoyed a punch-up with some of the local fellas, and this subsequently led to the police, the RUC, being summoned. All hell was about to be, or not to be, unfurled and unleashed.

It was to be.

The cops went in first.

After a second, a bar stool exploded with a roar, smashing through the window. We flinched backwards, cringing. Then a bigger object found its way out of a second window — a bloody huge wheelie bin! The rioters appeared in the doorway. The police gave way from the onslaught. The rioters were winning!

"Outta the fucking way!" screamed one guy!

"Fuck the pigs, man! SS, RUC!" yelled another, chanting the hatred.

"Oh, fuck, they're got dogs!" exclaimed another.

They were all brandishing improvised weapons from the bar and various other missiles: beer bottles, wheelie bins, knives, spoons — anything, really.

We turned off *The Predator*. This was infinitely more entertaining.

The cops regrouped like a Roman Legion, and we heard helicopters from above. Holy apocalypse now! Oh, the horror! The horror!

Searchlights sought out villains in the darkness! Police dogs sought out balls and testicles! Helicopters! The rioters even tried to light a wheelie bin and chuck it at the police. Someone must have given the order to use lethal force because I saw one officer brandishing a handgun, bringing it out as a warning.

"Oh, bloody hell!" Robert said.

After the cop pulled out his weapon, the crowd fell back slightly. They began to slowly but surely simmer down before completely fizzling out.

"Oh, thank God above!" said Mrs M in shock and awe. "No one got killed." She bit her top lip.

"Well, it's over now, Mum," Paul reassured her, hugging her shoulder.

Mrs. M said it best when she quipped,

"That was better than an episode of *The Bill*!" She went to sit down on her seat.

"Who's for tea?" Frederick giggled. "Oh, guys, that was so cool."

Heather just shrugged and sat down on the sofa bed.

"Yes please, matey, I'll have one!" I said to Paul. "Bunch up, Heather!" I added, sitting down beside her.

We turned on the TV again, just in time to hear Arnie Schwarzenegger saying,

"If it bleeds, we can keel it!"

Just a typical Friday night in Lisburn town…

"You foreign Devil, Johnny-San!" the blonde daimyo shouted.

'I've got your picture of me and you

You wrote 'I love you'

I wrote 'me too'

I sit there staring and there's nothing else to do

Oh it's in colour

Your hair is brown

Your eyes are hazel

And soft as clouds

I often kiss you when there's no one else around

I've got your picture, I've got your picture

I'd like a million of you all 'round myself

I want a doctor to take your picture

So I can look at you from inside as well

You've got me turning up and turning down

And turning in and turning 'round

I'm turning Japanese

I think I'm turning Japanese

I really think so

Turning Japanese

I think I'm turning Japanese

I really think so

I'm turning Japanese

I think I'm turning Japanese

I really think so

Turning Japanese

I think I'm turning Japanese

I really think so!"

(Lyrics by The Vapours)

Marty Møller chuckled as he rolled the dice.

It started when Marty lent me his copy of *Shogun* by James Clavell. It was then that my intrigue for the Japanese culture began. It was a superb book and, lo and behold, a great board game to boot.

Marty's interest in all things Japanese came about when he went to Japan with the Adventure Scouts for some worldwide scout jamboree thingy, and was subsequently placed with a ninja family of samurai warriors for two weeks. Thus, the seed was planted.

There was me, Paul Malone, Alan McC, Robert Malone, the Munnisher, and Stewart Reido. We were all sitting cross-legged on the floor in a circle, and getting deep vein thrombosis even before it became popular. But Marty insisted we should sit this way in order to fully appreciate the whole Japanese experience. Curse his Japanese ways! The next thing we knew, we would be drinking rice wine and using chopsticks — and we had neither! But we did have the number to one of the greatest Chinese restaurants in Lisburn! Maxums.

At this point, we were upstairs back in the hallowed portals of Outer Limits, 47 Bridge Street, Lisburn. It was the Summer of 1990. There were comics and all things *Manga*, and a certain addictive and sleep-depriving Japanese board-game named Shogun! And then some.

Quite suddenly, appearing almost out of nowhere, was a Japanese wind instrument warbling around us… then,

"*Gong!*"

"Holy frag," I said to Marty. I adjusted my legs from the lotus position into a more fashionable (ie comfortable) sitting position. "My armies suck ass, peasants, samurai, and old women!"

Then suddenly, a rift in time, a whirlpool sucked us into a different reality. We were transported by the mighty cosmic power back in time — to Feudal Japan!

"Perhaps," interjected the Munnisher, sniggering, "you are indeed an old woman!" His horse was burdened down with his considerable bulk and bigger hair and his armour shone blood-red in the sunset. He placed one hand on his hip and with the other he grabbed the horse's reins. He put his head back and laughed derisively.

Lord Robert Malone snorted, as did his horse.

 "What are your orders, Jay-San?"

Lord Robert of the Outer Limits, Commander of Legions of the Black Kiss,came to his aid, stopping his horse in front of Jay-San.

Jay-San's donkey brayed. Jay-San looked resplendent in his golden lion armour.

"I will take the Munn's head for that remark — and a portion of chicken-fried rice!" The donkey twitched his ears as an insect landed.

"Hai!" replied Lord Robert, bowing respectively.

"Charge! Yaa, mule! Yaa, mule!" Jay-San rode his faithful donkey Wilbur into the fray.

Like the water margin, the combined forces of the Shitting Poh attacked the Munnisher's keep.

There were seven fighting men against the forces of the Munnisher and one War Donkey. That would be enough to rival the warlord whose vast armies blotted out the setting sun.

The seven magnificent warriors included Jay-San, Marty-San, Paul-San, Alan McC, Robert-San, Reido-San, and some foot soldiers, some of whom were new recruits to the comic cause, ie Gary Machete and Andy Dillon. These were simply cannon fodder, the poor naive fools! Mwa ha ha ha!

And then the two forces collided. There was a clash of steel on steel. Donkey on Munn. Munn on donkey. Carnage ensued and then the Munn pulled out his card.

It was the Death Bringer Ninja Paul Andrews' card.

"Oh no!" we all said in unison. "Not the Death Bringer Ninja card!"

"Yeth! It is I, your arch nemesisth, the Ninja Andrews!" He brandished a ninja star and threw it at Wilbur.

Jay-San was too slow to deflect the incoming star with his sword. It struck smack between the eyes. Wilbur the war donkey was no more. Jay-San and Wilbur went down into the bloody dirt.

The Munnisher laughed victoriously.

"Ha! Your War Donkey was simply no match for my Ninja!"

"Nooo! Wil-burrrrr!" As Jay-San rose to feet, his voice became a growl, howling with a brutal animal rage. With a battle-cry to freeze blood, he launched himself through the enemy ranks with his companions not too far behind, chopping with their swords, punching and kicking with their martial art skills. Yet more ninjas appeared and hurled themselves toward the brave warriors of the Shitting Poh.

"Ninjas!" exclaimed Paul-San. "They're everywhere!"

"I hate ninjas!" said Jay-San, cleaving a ninja in the skull. The impact of the skull-splitting made a smiley face of blood on the wall.

"Ha! Take that Rorschach! That one is for Wilbur-San!"

The warriors were getting close to the enemies.

Then, suddenly,the intercom buzzed and we were pulled away from the cosmic rift and back into reality as the Chinese food was delivered.

We all ate heartily that evening. A great feast ensued. We drank flagons of ale; me, orange juice. We laughed till the setting of the sun and beyond. We toasted fallen comrades and a certain War Donkey.

"One day," I thought, "I will go to Japan."

We rescued Doctor Who.

Well, we tried!

You see, Paul had the ear of a local journalist geezer called Joe Fitzpatrick.

This guy saw Outer Limits in passing and popped in to have a chat and a scoop with Paul, which subsequently culminated in Paul getting his weekly half-page comic shop review in the Lisburn Ethos, a free local rag delivered to each home in Lisburn. *[Jay Note: Lisburn Ethos and The Ulster Starz shared the same premises and were situated directly opposite Greanz food fare — zombie central.]*

That was the idea at least.

I never got on with Joe. God rest his soul, he died some years ago, but I hope he's still writing on his big typewriter in the sky.

I'm sure the man was a decent guy, but he was bitterly sarcastic and smoked in my face and I can't abide that inconsideration.

Anyway, it came to pass that Doctor Who was going to be cancelled! Shock horror! We weren't gonna let this happen — not easily! Not our watch! No, Sir! So, it further came to pass that we were going to run a petition!

True to our word, we gathered a legion (okay, we scrounged up five fan boys — hey, it was short notice!) including Gavin Curly Hughes, Andy Creighton, (a real genuine guy who worked in the local record shop), Paul, Gary, and myself all

The Doctor Who fan club in Outer Limits. Courtesy of The Ulster Star, Lisburn
Left to right: Gavin Curly Hughes, Andy Creighton, Doctor Who, Paul Malone and Gary Malone

for this staged photograph. Joe arranged the shoot. I dressed up for the occasion; wearing my hat and long scarf, the image was complete.

I said to Joe, "Joe, this is a farce and you know it is! This phone here," I held it up, pointing at it, "isn't even connected to a phone line! How the frag are we gonna phone the British Broadcasting Corporation with it?"

"Well," he said, dragging his sentences out as per usual, almost like he had haemorrhoids.

"In this... game... it's all about illusion, Jonathan. The public image, ummm, needs to be seen, not heard. Oh, that's just perfect. Hold that! There!" He gasped as the photographer took the picture.

The deed was done.

But then it also came to pass that Doctor Who was cancelled, with thanks due to Sylvester McCoy, who was, in my book, the crappiest, most dire and worst Doctor *ever*.

Then Trev Lyons came on the scene. This guy was a saint in a blue transit van. A friend of Paddy and Rick Black, he looked like a thin Roy Orbison. He became a friend to us all and, whenever we needed transportation, he was always there to help, a bit like Scooby Doo's Mystery Machine! I baptised his van, naming it "The Transit of Doom!" We all piled in, a full load of girl and boy fans; well, at least ten people. If the fuzz stopped us, we were done for!

We had some great nights out in the back of Saint Trevor Lyons' Transit of Doom. All he needed was a cravat and the image would be complete. Yoinks and Jinkies! Some memorable evenings out included The Batman Tim Burton trip and Tullymore Forest Park. Late at night, Trev took us out to the forest park and the stars were just amazing!

"My God," I said as we lay on top of his van, "The sky's full of stars!"

"Johnny," said Marty! "Harry Harrison and Terry Pratchett are over here signing at the Queen's University Mekon Convention!"

"Oh, really?" I said. "We are there!"

Meanwhile, true believers, back in the summer of 1990 we found transport to Belfast via the local Ulsterbus service. Marty had brought his mate Andrew along. I have to tell you, the guy had no personality whatsoever. He was a fan of Terry Pratchett. Says it all, *really*. I, on the other hand, was a big fan of Harry Harrison, as was Marty. I adored Harry's work and had done ever since I watched *Soylent Green* with my Dad who, like me, was into science fiction. He had a vast library of pulp sci-fi novels upstairs in the spare room, ranging from Asimov to Harrison and beyond. I would peruse his collection occasionally. *The Stainless Steel Rat* books were favourites of mine. My Dad read *Discworld*. His verdict? He thought it was boring nonsense. I read a short story of Terry's about Death and, as luck would have it, father and son had fallen from the same tree. I thought it was boring nonsense too. I agreed with my Dad: Harry's work was legendary, and then some.

When we got to Queen's, all the usual Goths, cheese rangers and anoraks were there in abundance. Andy pulled his anorak hood off and scanned the area.

"There's Terry!"

Yawn, I thought.

Terry Pratchett, creator of *Discworld*, was wearing a big floppy hat. Says it all, *really*. I shook his hand, introduced myself to the man, and looked him in the eye somewhat suspiciously, and said,

"Where's Harry, Terry?"

"You wascal!" he said in his trademark soft lisp. He continued, "I'm here to signth my *Discworld* novelsth! Do you want me to signth anything for you?" he asked.

"You've got to be joking!" I scoffed. There was a brief hesitation and I spotted Harry.

"Thanks Tel! Come on, Marty, let's hoof it!" I pulled Marty's sleeve and off we went, Marty and me, to see the main attraction, leaving Tel and Andy to it, both looking bemused.

Harry Harrison. What an honour! He looked a little like Father Christmas but without the red suit. He had the same white beard and glasses.

I introduced myself to this illustrious sci-fi legend!

He said, "What can I sign for you men?"

Between us, Marty and I had a wide variety of novels for him to sign, from the *Rat* books, to my treasured possession, the *Technicolor*™ *Time Machine*.

"Oh, where did you find this, Jonathan?" Harry asked, referring to the latter and raising his bushy eyebrows. He pushed his glasses down to examine it more closely.

"I found it in a second-hand bookstore in Lisburn, Harry. Can we ask you something? What will you call your next *Rat* book? We've read them all!"

"Mmmm," he paused to consider, picking up his pen, bringing it to his mouth and nibbling on the end as he thought. He briefly wiggled it between his pearly whites before taking it out to examine, then he looked up at me from his glasses, and said in his American drawl,

"Why, Jonathan, ah believe ah'll call mah next book, *The Stainless Steel Rat Sings The Blues!*

And he did — and I bought it.

"NANA NANA NANA NANA — NANA NANA NANA NANA — BATMAN!" I wrote on a big whack of paper. I stuck it in the window of Outer Limits using a blob of blue tack on each corner. My trusty black marker pen had helped me to proclaim that *Batman*, the Tim Burton extravaganza, was in The Old Vic in Belfast — and we were there!

Spinning round The Outer Limits logo at extreme velocity and fading in and out like the Batman logo!

It took two vehicles, the Transit of Doom and Robert's white Panda car, for us to reach our destination, including not only our gang but all the punters from the comic shop who wanted to go. It was deemed necessary for Curly Gavin Hughes to be transported in the boot of Robert's car. He was the smallest and least valuable comicshopian. Indeed, he volunteered for the mission. Sucker. *[Jay Note: a comicshopian is a denizen of a comic shop.]*

"Oh, please, Mrs Hughes, don't tell Childline we kidnapped your first-born of spring and sold him into slavery down in New Orleans!"

Twack! Kapow! Tallywhacker!

So we all disembarked from our respective transports into the nearest car park, and thence onto Robinson's bar, wherein we partook of refreshments, some of the alcoholic kind, though not myself, of course.

Outside, I noticed a tramp. The poor geezer was thin and had a beard with something lurking within. Lice, no doubt. Nice, I thought. But, in this day and age, a guy with a beard like that could use a break and so I popped a quid into his tin cup. He mumbled something indiscernible but tipped his cloth cap in respect.

"No need to thank me, citizen, action is my only reward." I stood with my hands on my hips, looking far into the distance.

It was the Grosvenor Road — we had reached our destination! The Old Vic was ours for the taking! *Grunt! Thwack! Kapow!*

But our rival comic shop in Belfast, the Tallywhacker, had beaten us to it! We saw Malarkey and Jon there in front of us. Malarkey the Goth had dyed his hair green and put on white face-paint. A sad imitation of the Joker, no less.

We were in for a long wait. Our tramp friend had followed us. I decided we should all have a whip-round for the Yoda lookalike, even including the perfect strangers, who were queuing with us.

"Come on! Let's help this guy out," I said, rattling his wee can. "You! You look rich! Are you a Christian?"

The woman was taken aback and nervously said, "No!"

I condemned her right there and then.

"Then may God forgive you! For it is said it is easier to thread a camel through the eye of a needle than for a rich man to enter the kingdom of heaven!"

Richard the Munnisher said,

"Right on, brother!" with his fist clenched.

We raised about a tenner for Yoda. Yoda stumbled away through the traffic. Again, the queue got shorter. Soon after, we spotted Yoda again.

Ah good! I thought when I saw him clutching a bag — he'd bought himself food! Again, I guess I was young and innocent back then. Human nature does not quite work that way. To my dismay, he had gotten himself a huge carry-out of beer and he sat right there beside us, foaming at the mouth, leering at the lady who didn't give him any money.

I was so embarrassed. No one knew where to look. I think even someone called the police and Yoda was arrested for vagrancy. The last we saw, Yoda was in the back of Da Black Maria, on the way to the drunken tank.

The queue got shorter, and to quote Elwood P. Dowd in *Harvey*, "The evening wore on…"

The film was … expletive deleted.

Easter that year was excellent. Myself, Paddy and Paul Andrews decided to go on our pushbikes around the Mournes. Down through Ballynahinch, towards Downpatrick, around Ballynoe and onwards through the Mournes.

That was the plan, at least, and it worked surprisingly well. Well, when I say "surprisingly", I refer to the fact that we didn't expect the Death Bringer to last, but he did.

We all set out from the shop and Paul came out to wish us well. We had my tent, the Dew Master AD 150, check. A map, check. Food and money, double-check. Paddy, check. Myself, check again. Bikes and rucksacks, check and Paul Andrews, the Death Bringer — as the Sarge said to Henry, the mild-mannered janitor of *Hong Kong Phooey* (number one super guy fame),

"Maybe!"

"Jay, Andrews, he'll never make it up that hill," said Paddy, he the look-alike of the Simple Minds lead singer Jim Kerr. He added, "He'll end up turning back!"

I looked back despondently. I waved with one hand on my handlebar. I called back,

"Come on, Paul!"

His voice replied in the wind, puffing his lungs out,

 "I'm goith asth fast asth I can, Johnny!" Poor Paul. Years of nicotine and alcohol abuse had taken their toll on his plump frame. He told us,

"The reasonth I want to go with you guyths is my mum and I had an argument and she threw me out!"

Our journey led us to the hills of Dromore and Down. We saw some sheep giving birth to lambs. The circle of life. It was beautiful to behold, especially with mint sauce. Mmmm. Lamb chops, my favourite kind of chop. After pausing to watch this spectacle, salivating, we pressed on.

Our first port of call was Ballynoe Stone Circle, an ancient stone-aged Celtic monument, and that's where we intended to make camp. The previous Solstice, Paul took me, Ellen and Heather Hamilton up to the said ring for a maiden sacrifice in Robert's Panda car. Our fair maidens, however, were not interested in our masculine ways. The evening ended with Robert's Panda car going up in flames as a result of his fuel pump overheating in the summer heat. Nevertheless, Paul heroically saved our hides by beating it out with a trusty towel.

So, the story continues with us making camp in a secluded field inside the ancient monument, hiding our bikes close by. We walked over a stile. I always remember my dad teaching me this wee rhyme on his knee:

"I met a crooked man, who wore a crooked hat, who walked a crooked mile, who found a crooked penny, on a crooked stile." And, with that memory in mind, every time I walked over a stile into a field or country road, I would fondly remember his words with a smile.

We all walked down the dusty lane, chatting amongst ourselves, kicking gravel, and pulling the heads of grass stems that we plucked off.

"Holy pluck!" we exclaimed when we turned the corner and we saw the local bar, which was — I kid you not — named The Slaughtered Lamb, twinned, of course, with the pub in *American Werewolf in London*. Inside the said establishment was all the standard guff to bring American tourists to these shores: peat fires, old yokes, a wolf's head on top of the bar, buxom bar staff, an Irish folk band singing in the corner, and all that old-time charm. Ker ching!

"Mmmm, this looks okay!"

There was a deathly silence as everyone stopped and looked at us. Everyone, including the wolf's head on top of the bar, it seemed. After a long drawn-out silence, the music and revelry renewed as we sat down cautiously.

"What can I get you gentlemen?" the buxom barmaid asked as she stooped down to reveal her chest.

Paddy said with a wolfish grin, "Could we have two of those please?" pointing over her shoulder towards the Guinness on tap.

"I will have an orange juice, hold the ice," I said with my eyes wide open.

Paul Andrews hit the slot machine. Gambling was amongst his many vices. He always had the luck of the Death Bringer on his side. He always hit the jackpot... That Death Bringer sure could play a mean pinball!

"Come on, Paul, it's time for us to leave!" I said, just as the slot machine poured its guts out.

"Hold on, Johnny, gimme a thecond to collecth my winningsth!" he drooled, filling his pockets full to the brim with pound coins.

I think the local yokels, the country bumpkins, were outraged by the pluck of the Devil. They were forming a lynch mob. We got out by the skin of our teeth.

Meanwhile, back at our camp, we put up my tent and cracked open a tin of beans, putting them on the camp stove. Later that evening, when the Death Bringer, Paddy and myself settled down to sleep, Paul, who was sleeping in the middle of our three-man tent, let rip with the most foul, ripe, Guinness and beans smelling bottom burp I have ever had the misfortune to smell in my entire life — and I've smelt CS gas.

He started to snore. And then we were subjected to his death-breath.

This overwhelming stench filled our tent. Paddy's farts weren't as bad. I admit mine weren't too fragrant either. But the combination of tobacco, Guinness and beans turned Andrews into a lethal evil force of doom. No small wonder I nicknamed him the Death Bringer.

Dawn came slowly.

"Holy frag!" I shouted. "What the bloody hell?"

A large form nudged the side of the tent! We all climbed out in our socks.

It was a horse! It trotted away, slowly. I love horses but had never ridden one. It was one of my ambitions.

One day I will, I mused to myself.

Soon enough, it was time to get on the bikes again!

Easter Saturday, we followed the coastal route to Kilkeel and camped overnight in Mourne Park. Easter Sunday, we headed home, up through Hilltown to Rathfriland. Paul Andrews did survive; I admit I was surprised and even admired him for his efforts. He took my tent home with him to show his mum. I never saw the Dew Master AD 150 again.

Soon, that was when I started puking up pizzas and fainting at home.

Hey, I am a young guy, I would think to myself. It's nothing to worry about. But then I collapsed in the downstairs toilet. I faded out. My dad caught my arm as I fell, my eyes now white as they rolled back in their sockets. It was as if I was having a seizure.

"Relax, Dad," I later told him, shrugging it off. "I will be fine! I'm always fine! I am running everywhere and cycling! No time! No time! No time…"

I bought a fragging lethal weapon: an Excalibur crossbow. I had saved up for it and added to it from my TA wages. I purchased it from the aptly named "Gun and Tackle" shop from a dodgy geezer. This was to be my Mega-Plan, conceived in the forest on my TA expedition. By this stage, I was getting slightly paranoid about certain people. I was in control. I was going to go native. Walk the land. After all, I had my territorial training. There was absolutely nothing to worry about.

I felt the world was ending and it did. For me.

When Paul saw the crossbow, he said,

"Holy fuck, Jay! Are you mad?"

But, again, it was nothing to worry about. I was in control and had my Mega-Plan.

"Relax, my best friend. I am going to go native. Walk the land, I have my territorial training. It's nothing to worry about."

Or was it?

Paul Malone, my best friend. He is the man; that's all I can say.

Meanwhile, back to that rainy day. The rain started to die down and fizzle out.

"Hey, Paul," I said. "Look, the sun's coming out."

Truly, at the Outer Limits shop, we forged friendships of the rarest and most unique type. The comic shop still lives on in all our imaginations. It never really shut its doors. Sure, it's changed hands, the premises, that is, but to me, 47 Bridge Street will always be Outer Limits.

It's a comic shop, yeah!

Dona, by Jonathan

CHAPTER SEVENTEEN: DEATH AND GLORY

It was October, 1991.

"Sure. We can hire an Ulsterbus. Whack a sign on the front saying, "Hell via The Astrozombies 666". It could go to Richhill, Armagh and the Old Station House. My bro-in-law Martin Campbell won't mind if we use it to put on a fraggin' mind-blowing concert for all the youth of Lisburn for Hallowe'en," I said. And I did.

I was dying.

Somewhere, deep in the cells of my body, there was something lurking, a twisting malevolent force. I put on my trademark Lobo face-paint in Martin and Heather's bathroom, but my hands shook with all the adrenaline running through my body. I almost collapsed and fainted right then and there and I was forced to clench onto the sink for support. I had a bottle of antiseptic TCP. I took a swig and gargled. I retched into the sink. I looked at myself in the mirror and towards the back of my throat. It looked like something out of Hell, all green and pustules. I pulled myself together and stared deep into the mirror. Not good, but hey, not bad either.

The show must go on.

I managed to get the face-paint on. I wrapped my black cloak around me, and went through the house and on to the station, almost like how Béla Lugosi would have done. It was legendary.

"Johnny! Johnny! Johnny!" they all intoned with a rapturous applause. They wanted my blood, and I gave it to them.

First on the bill was Gavin Curly Hughes's band, if you could call them that, the "Brand New Spanking Badgers." I could have easily conjured up a pun about that name, but I didn't. Oh, the cruel irony of youth. Anyway, they played some lame-ass songs, which didn't go down too well and, soon enough, it was up to me to save the day. I shoved the Badgers off their depressing stage.

My fellow Astrozombies were Richard the Munnisher Munn, guitarist, Keith Møller, the bassist with attitude, and Derek Lockhart, the drummer from the seventh level of Hell, and together we were the ultimate Misfits and Danzig tribute band.

Left to right: Paul Andrews, John Fisher Astrozombie and Keith Møller

"We are the Astrozombies, and I want your skulls! I need your skulls!" I grated through my trusty mic.

The crowd roared in appreciation. The station became a mosh pit from the seventh level of Hades, complete with head-bangers all around. And me, in the midst of them, like some masked demon, half-naked and dying.

"It's a long way back from Hell! And you don't want to go there, friend!"

We tried, for the first time in our repertoire-grimoire, "She rides", fooling around with Dona, my girlfriend at that time.

There is always one beta that wants to usurp the alpha in the pack. In fact, there were two that evening: one was Alan McColonicIrrigation, and another runt, whose name I can't remember at this time. This wee dweeboid kept bumping into me and it was, quite frankly, most annoying.

"Bouncers, destroy him!"

We climaxed with, "It's got to be! Got to be a twist of Cain!" Rick, Deewik and

Left to right: John Fisher Astrozombie, Alan, Gary, Dave, Colin, Rob and Richard

Keith exploded their instruments in a sub-atomic fusion of rock.

Soon, it was time to leave the gig. I arranged for the Ulsterbus to pick us up at the witching hour. The sky was full of stars, and the latrine, which was the station beyond the platform, was full of people urinating. I think someone fell in. It could have been the Death Bringer Paul Andrews, our lighting co-ordinator, who had the unfortunate and somewhat mind-numbing task of constantly rubbing two dimmer switches with his two front paws to produce the desired lighting effect! So, all aboard!

We set sail into the November country, journeying through the apple trees that litter Armagh, into the darkness. I laid my head against one of the windows, looking out into the wilderness and the stars above, thinking. Dona laid her head beside mine. She slept until we saw the lights of Hallowe'en town approaching. Sweet Lisburn.

"Everyone out! Last stop!" The bus driver looked at me and just smiled.

Everyone had lifts home to their respective dwellings. I had left my bike at the shop. I kissed Dona passionately and she went home with her friend.

I decided to walk a little with Richard Munn. He thought that the Samhain Mayhem gig was his best guitar performance, undoubtedly, ever. And it really was.

I cycled home. My mum always left the back door open. I locked the back door, and put on the fluorescent lights. My mother (who is very wise) put out a little bread, some salt in a wee dish, a glass of water and a candle every Old Souls' Night. I stared at it, just for a while, and then I put out the lights. The candlelight flicked onto my retinas and I tiptoed up to my bed. I collapsed onto it.

I was dying.

The following day, I went to see my GP in Belfast. He gave me a check-up. He looked down my throat, gave me a penicillin prescription, and said,

"You will be fine, Jonathan. If the symptoms persist, I'll give you something stronger, and here are some seasickness tablets for you to keep the nausea down."

I thanked him, and shook his hand. I trusted doctors back then.

After work in Bryson House, I felt ill, and so I asked my Line Manager, Gary Robb, if I could go home early. I took the train to Lisburn and cycled home. I was going to ask mum if she could get my prescription.

I was burning. Imagine the most indescribable pain and multiply it a million times, and you still simply can't comprehend. It was like walking through fire naked. I collapsed onto the sofa in the living room, crying and writhing about. I was breathing rapidly.

"Mummy, what's happening to me?"

My poor parents didn't have a clue. Mother helped me up to bed.

I had a dream that night. But it wasn't really a dream: It was like walking into a different reality…

There was a tunnel with an orange light source. It was the far future. I know this because there were all these strange uniforms. I saw my reflection in a pool of water. I was a tunnel worker, and there were all these people — old and young — shouting at me to hold the tunnel open. It was collapsing while I was trying to hold it up with my arms. Darkness followed shortly afterwards.

There was darkness all around him. He couldn't see anything, and this disturbed him greatly. He could, however, hear machines. What sort of machines? There were smells too: the smell of a hospital, he thought. In the distant past, he had experienced various ailments: cuts and bruises, which required visitations, the sort of things all small boys have. Then he recognised the sound the machines made. Life support machines.

"Where the hell am I?"

The machine continued to make a sucking noise, louder and louder, almost deafening, intermingled with screams — or was that laughter mocking him?

He was in pain. He tried to move but he found he could not. The pain wouldn't allow it. He heard voices and faces were swimming in and out of reality. One voice said,

"The experiment continues."

The other voice said with a touch of menace,

"The drugs will take effect soon. He won't remember this."

It was like Hell. This place was called the citadel, or the facility to some. All he could make out in those moments of lucidity, before the drugs took a hold of his system, was that others were in the room with him.

The room had horrible lime-green and yellow painted walls. There was a crack in the ceiling from where a fluorescent light hung, caked in dead insects. The light flickered incessantly and buzzed like a deranged wasp. The smell made him vomit and an orderly with a white uniform, stained with puss, blood and urine, attended him. The orderly had a scraggly blonde beard, bad smoke-stained teeth, and he had a nametag that read "Peter Meaner."

He said, "That's great clone scum. That will brighten the place up a bit!" His complexion was a mass of greasy blackheads, which were beginning to form as puss-filled zits on his neck.

"Now, now, Peter; that won't do at all. These creatures are our guests at the facility," the meaner cruel voice said.

He was beginning to become more aware, stronger now. He looked up at his tormentors, the three men in the room. Two doctors and the orderly. One doctor had red hair and a beard, Doctor Sorrow; the other looked more sinister and had black hair and dark eyes, Doctor Deadhill.

He mouthed a weak question,

"Why?"

"Peter!" the red-haired doctor commanded. "Sedate the incarcerator clone immediately or you'll be next for the genetic baths!"

"Noooo!" the incarcerator screamed in agony, thrashing wildly on the bed. "Go to hell!" He started to pull the tubes out from his nose. From his arms, blood and mucus spurted everywhere.

"Restrain him!" the dark doctor demanded.

Soon, it was done. Peter plunged the needle into the right arm of the incarcerator. Peter grinned, a horrible yellow-teeth grimace, his foul-smelling breath overpowering him. Leering into his face, Peter hissed in a cold evil whisper,

"You filthy animal, you are already here." The incarcerator involuntarily lost control of his bladder and bowels as he went into spasm. Urine seeped onto the ground in a warm trickle.

"Oh, that's just wonderful. More mess to clean up!" Peter lit a cigarette.

Night came in the citadel. The screams started and were getting closer, like some gruesome reverberation that chilled the soul. In his chamber, he waited for the inevitable. Strapped to his bed, he began to come round. Looking around his cell, he could only see a door. How he yearned to walk out that door, to the real world beyond. But that was just a fantasy. This hell-hole world was his now.

Then the door was flung open with a loud crash.

"Medicine! Medicine time!" An old nurse cackled and screeched at the top of her voice. "Hello, deary! Time! Time! Medicine! Medicine time!"

Her name was Harriet Hatchet Face. Her face was covered in warts. She was an ugly, withered old woman with cracked lips and ancient red lipstick.

"Sleep well, deary. You will need it!" She gave the incarcerator some medicine from her drug trolley. "Swallow, deary!"

Slowly, like through a fog, some men in white suits entered the cell. They all wore masks and dirty gloves, dripping with the effluent of some gore.

"Is this the next one, nurse?"

They wiped and blew their noses on the incarcerator's gown.

"Why, certainly!"

The last thing the incarcerator heard that night was the sound of chainsaws and sucking noises, during which time the anaesthetic gave him hallucinogenic dreams — but was he dreaming? He saw visions whilst he was under: he saw his right leg being severed, the blood and cartilage spilling everywhere, spurting out like a hot ejaculation; he saw his left leg ripped asunder, the doctors all the while discussing the hot number at reception, and the intentions one had with the conservatory he was building in his garden.

"Hey, Bob," one doctor said leeringly. "Did you manage to check out the cutie clone at reception? I'd love her to swap DNA with me!" He howled and grunted like a farmyard animal.

The other doctor snorted his agreement and said, "Yeah, you and me both!"

"How's your conservatory, Bob?"

"Oh, it's coming along!" he sniggered. "How's the patient?"

"Don't worry about him, he's nothing."

In the morning, he was half a man.

"You bastards! You fuckers! You wank-stains! What have you done to me?" The incarcerator cried weakly. He sobbed, as he looked down at the space where his legs had once been.

"Being a clone, you have little rights, my friend," Doctor Sorrow said, looking down at him like a piece of meat. He added with a grin on his evil face, "We pure humans require spare parts, if you will. After the great catastrophe, when the ozone layer failed in the final years of the twenty-first century, you simply became fodder for us." He licked his lips, saliva drooling from his moustache.

"What right do you have to tell us what we can and cannot do, you sick, twisted fuck? You freak!" the incarcerator retorted and spat at Doctor Sorrow.

"Still a bit of fight there, I see? But, sadly for you, it is you who is the freak!" he said, laughing. The Doctor added now with menacing tones, "We shall see after the next treatment!"

Into the room came Doctor Deadhill along with Peter. They immediately put an oxygen mask on the incarcerator.

"Breathe deep and think of clone," Peter said, grinning menacingly.

Nightmares — but this was the daytime, wasn't it? But what was time to the incarcerator? Time meant nothing to him in this place of suffering. He tried to dream when he was asleep. In one dream, he thought he imagined he was in a far distant future land where the grass was green and the air was clean, and he drank from pools that were clear, using his hands as a cup. He drank long and deep until he was satisfied. There were flowers and wildlife; everything he could have wanted was in that land. But he was lonely and so alone. When he shouted, the echoes returned to him to taunt him. Now, time to him was simply a long tunnel to crawl through in the darkness. Tunnels didn't usually have lights at the end; they were dark. And he was in Hell.

After the next treatment, he had no arms. The doctors removed his humanity. He was only a torso being fed intravenously. And, after going completely insane, they took his skull and gouged out his eyeballs. Then his vocal chords were harvested, and then his eardrums.

He could not speak. He could not see. He could not hear. But, by then, he did not care…

I woke up the following morning, covered in sweat. I washed and shaved myself. Breakfast was waiting downstairs for me in the kitchen: cornflakes, a thick heel of Ormo bread toasted, and mummy and daddy smiling.

Heaven.

"How are you feeling now, son?" My father asked.

"A bit better, Dad, thanks." I chomped with my mouth full. "Mummy, did you get the penicillin? Did you phone the surgery?"

"Yes to both your questions, Jonathan."

I took the penicillin.

The following evening, I went to look out our back and gazed up at the night sky with my trustee binoculars. I went up to Ballymacash Primary School, where there is shelter from the street lamps.

All the usual favourites were up: Orion, Canis Major, Sirius and the Pleiades star cluster. And, oh my fragging God. My skin shivered and all the hairs on my body stood up on end. What was that? It was the Aurora Borealis, the Northern Lights! It was amazing. It was like a sheet of pure energy waving from horizon to horizon. Waving, undulating, across the sky. Photographs don't do it justice. This was the real thing. The sky cackled and shimmered. I felt humbled, and even felt sorry for those poor fools who were watching their soap operas on the television all over this area of Lisburn. It was, without a fragging doubt, the most beautiful thing I have ever seen in my entire life, and I was completely in awe.

The months passed. Christmas 1991 was a good time, aside from my ailing health and a few other visits to the Doctor in Belfast. Apart from that, however, I was in good spirits. That was the last Christmas we had as what anyone would call a "normal" family unit. Mummy's turkey dinner and Dad playing "Give us a clue" on Old Year's Night with his friends and neighbours was fantastic. Everyone was in the living room smoking, laughing and drinking.

Months passed, I developed a really sexy bronze colour all over my skin. You would have sworn that I'd been on holiday in the Orient. Mum put it down to all the cycling and running I had been doing.

Work was good at Bryson House. I was a trainee graphic designer — and a pretty good one, at that. I have fond memories of that place. There was big man Mike, Neal, Alex, Eddie the photographer and Gary Robb. One day, Mike and myself were browsing around the streets of Belfast on our lunch hour, when I just happened to look in the window of the Games Workshop. A flash of light glimmered in the sunlight. There, in the window, I saw these two words: Space Crusade.

Holy frag! I thought to myself and, in a flash, money was tendered — sold! I had Space Crusade!

"The guys from the comic shop will love this!" I told Mike enthusiastically. "Yesss!"

And they did.

Space Crusade was exactly what it said on the tin — or the cardboard rather! It was a board game with a stunning difference. There were six teams of Space Marines to combat in a space station. We usually played in Rick Black's house with his flirty sister looking over our shoulders. One night, for entertainment purposes, he put his cat, Sooty, in the microwave oven and set it to nuke, just for a second, mind you. Kids, do not try this at home! Oh, the fun we had playing that game until the early hours of the morning.

Early March 1992 and we all went to see the Red Hot Chilli Peppers in the Ulster Hall. They rocked ass.

It was in Easter that year that everything changed. Everything.

It was April the thirtieth. Mum's cousins, Edna and Mabel, came to visit. We all had a bowl of mummy's homemade soup for lunch. I wasn't feeling too well. I had a bad bout of diarrhoea that morning and was in my pyjama bottoms that day. They had strange paisley swirling patterns in mauve. I was wearing a "nuke me slowly" T-shirt from *Marshal Law*, bought from Outer Limits (it's a comic shop, yeah!) and my white slippers, which had seen better days.

I was on the wee two-seater in our living room. It was a beautiful spring day, and mummy had the living room window open for me. I was feeling a little warm and the fresh air did me the power of good.

Mummy's cousins hugged me and said,

"Hope you feel a bit more like yourself soon, Jonathan. Take care!"

That evening, I vomited the soup. My mother (who is very wise) gave me the tablets the doctor had given me — the seasickness tablets. More vomiting ensued, and then more diarrhoea.

Then I said to lovely mother,

"I love you, mummy. I need the toilet again. Would you help me?" I was in the upstairs bathroom.

Then I went to bed, but I couldn't sleep. I managed to go downstairs, disorientated. I managed to make it through the living room door. And that was where everything went white. I said,

"Hell's bells," and then choked and fainted. I curled up into a foetal position on the floor.

And I died.

From what I can gather, when my parents saw me like that, all hell broke loose. My mother (who is very wise) did her best to resuscitate me as my father phoned for an ambulance.

I was dead.

But I was still fighting.

There was a kernel of life remaining. A dying ember of fire in my brain stream. You may call it the soul — some people do.

A woman blew upon this ember. This woman brought me into the world and her name is Emma Eileen Magee Fisher, my mother. Yes, a woman's love brought me back from the brink of death. My mother, who is very wise indeed.

I had a massive infection. The doctors didn't have a clue what had caused it. My brain was starved of oxygen during the period of time before the ambulance came and brought me to the Lagan Valley Hospital where they stabilised my condition. I was then moved to the Royal Victoria in Belfast where I spent a number of months in a coma.

More whiteness.

More doctors.

Physiotherapists.

Then, a breakthrough. A doctor made a culture of my blood and decided to pump me full of steroids, specifically a drug called cortisone. Soon afterwards, they made their diagnosis.

I had suffered an Addisonian insult to my brain, otherwise known as Addison's disease.

In the background, everyone was trying to help me live. In this world in which we co-exist with local germs, bugs, and viruses all wanting to kill you, eat your flesh, these wee bastards had tried it on with me and *failed*.

More whiteness.

Sensation.

A light.

A sound.

I could make out a nurse's uniform. There was heat. I was in an ambulance on my way to the Lagan Valley Hospital. I was spun around in a strange bed. I felt a bump and a lot of commotion and rushing about. I was in a hospital lift. I felt something. What's this nausea? I felt sick. I tried to raise my head but I couldn't manage it. I tried to move my legs but I couldn't. I tried to move my arms but I couldn't. I tried to speak but I couldn't. I tried to scream but I couldn't. I was wrapped up like an Egyptian mummy. Cocooned for my journey down the Nile to the Pyramids. My throat had something in it I could not think about. Oh, that's how I breathe? I gasped for air. There was a machine I could not make out now with my peripheral vision. Another sense was trying to return. My brain was beginning to "reboot."

Then I saw another taller nurse, one with blonde hair. She said,

"There he is!" The nurse brought my parents and David. I smiled at them.

They all crowded around my bed. David made the funny face that I liked. My mum kissed my forehead and I started to cry.

And so began my new life.

The nurse's name was Gail. How did I know that? I could read her nametag, despite it being a bit blurry and jumbled up. I felt that this was somehow important. I could read! Boy, just making one word tired me out. I wanted to sleep, but the physiotherapists had other ideas.

There was this man and his family in the ward opposite me. He was walking with a stick. I think my dad recognised him from the Royal Legion. He was called Harry. Harry Cain.

A lot more commotion ensued. I was shuttled into a side ward, a wee room of my own. My father said his goodbyes to Harry and his family and then some visitors began to arrive: my sisters; Dona came but she was shooed away — family only; David, my brother; my mum. They all turned the side ward into a converted parallel bedroom in the old house. All family photos, posters, teddy bears, even a stuffed Garfield toy with a "Hello, Sailor" cap my brother had bought me, and a plush Gremlin Gizmo from the film that I loved so much, and something else which my sister Sharon got me — an inflatable balloon pumpkin face. I hated it. It was evil. I could see its evil maw grinning at me while it turned in the air.

I started moaning in pain. I couldn't tell them how much distress I was in. This was around the stage that I found I could click my tongue around the roof of my mouth and communicate pain and distress.

At set periods of time, I was rolled over to prevent bedsores. My drip was changed, as was my feeding tube through my nose to my stomach and a new bandage for my trachea. Oh, and we cannot forget the catheter in my wing wang doodle.

I wasn't a pretty sight.

I always prided myself on my body. I worked out. I cycled. I ran for miles upon miles everywhere. I swam. I was a sex machine, I made love for hours. All that, it seems, is gone.

But what the hell! I was still alive, yeah?

Now the torture truly began with physiotherapy. There were four physiotherapists. They came every day after I was changed and drained. They had a machine. I remembered something! From a book. Ray Bradbury's *Fahrenheit 451*. Montag's wife Mildred. She had her stomach pumped after an overdose.

"God, who were those men? I never saw them before in my life! God, who are these women? I have never seen them before in my life!" What are they doing to me? They were draining my lungs because I had pneumonia, amongst other things.

Then they put me in another bed, which they had from the gym. It was a new kind of pain, like being pulled apart on a torture rack. I managed a tiny scream, a loud moaning. I turned to mummy and Sharon, begging them with my eyes not to leave. They stayed and held my burning hands. For the first few days, they remained, but the head physiotherapist, Margaret, suggested they should go and let the girls do their job. I was scared and frightened, and had no idea what they were going to do to me.

In other cases, the prospect of four attractive women pulling me apart would be any guy's dream but these women had a way of shattering a guy's dream. They were physiotherapists. There was Margaret, Karolyn, a girl with an Irish name, which I couldn't translate with my damaged software (she had striking curly ginger hair), and another young physio; all of them treated me in my room. Margaret was amazing. She had kind eyes and a soft voice. She held my head and my neck whilst the other three did their dastardly deeds on my limbs, stretching my back and my arms and legs that were still entombed in plaster. This, I was told, was to prevent contractures and it would help my limbs to straighten again.

Then, one day, they tried to stand me up. This meant a lot of hard work for them and a greater effort from me. They had a mirror in the ward. Margaret and the girls helped me to look into the mirror whilst holding my head as I had no muscle control. I was their marionette, a puppet on a string. She said,

"Who's that good-looking green-eyed guy in the mirror, hmmm?"

I was beginning to mouth silent words.

I mouthed, "Me." I looked like something out of a Nazi concentration camp: I was like a skeleton, all gaunt and thin, with a big bushy beard. No one had dared to shave me in case I took an infection. I looked like hell.

Days later, Margaret and the team put me in a chair so that I could sit. An ordinary armchair. She kept trying to get my floppy head to balance itself — and finally it did! I was so happy! I laughed, or at least I tried to laugh! Everyone in the room was so overjoyed. Margaret brought my mum in. She was so pleased to see me laughing for the first time. I started to cry again.

Early one morning, a nurse from the x-ray unit with piercing blue eyes, blonde hair and an English accent came into my ward and stood looking down at me. She stroked my cheek gently and whispered,

 "You have beautiful eyes." Hello! This gave me a stirring down below. Still got it. I whispered,

"Thank you." I never saw her again.

The guys from Outer Limits came. Everyone came to visit me at one stage or another. They all came in pilgrimage to pay homage to their fallen leader. They brought cards, comics, progs and videos for me to watch on the television and the video player David had brought me from home. I watched *Star Trek* whilst the guys would take turns to read *Dune* by Frank Herbert, my favourite novel. My family also read *Dune* to me, but my sisters had no idea how to pronounce some of the words in the novel. I mean, how hard is it to pronounce "Kwistatz Haderach"? David brought me in *Lord of the Rings* radio play, which was dramatized on Radio 4.

The nights were horrible. Lagan Valley had one male nurse. His name was Trevor. He was a good nurse; I thought he was slightly effeminate. Every evening, he would come round to wish "the child" goodnight. He had halitosis (bad breath) and, one evening when he came to my ward, he leaned over me and I began to retch. I whispered,

"Go to hell! Go to hell!" and I tried to turn away from the pong. But Trevor said, "No I won't. I want you to get better and get out of this place!" Then I realised where I was and where he was.

In Lagan Valley Hospital, the closest place to hell I have ever been. But there were angels there too, some in the guise of a male nurse.

Once, my leg got trapped at the end of my bed! I clicked and moaned furiously for at least half an hour. Realistically, it could have been more, as my sense of time was totally fragged. Eventually, an old fusspot nurse came to investigate.

"What's all this clicking about?" she said harshly. "This won't do at all!" she scolded, saying, "I have patients in this ward that want to sleep!" She turned my bedside lamp off. And she added, "Go to sleep, young man, and enough of that infernal clicking! It sounds like a water tap!"

I was furious! My mum had written out some cue cards for the nurses, saying on them things like, "wash me, please", "turn my lamp on, please", "a drink of water, please" and "change my dressings, please." These cards were left out on the table because the buzzer to call the night staff was on the right side of the room on the wall.

My left hand was the more dominant one now. Fortunately for me, a nicer younger nurse heard the commotion and came into the ward and put the big light on.

"You poor thing! We'll help you!" And they did.

Soon after, the nurse who completely failed me, was transferred. I told mummy what happened in my ghost whisper. She told Trevor, the head nurse.

"No one treats my son like that!" She absolutely ate him alive.

Morning came slowly. I had to drink through a gauze strip in my neck. I did a smacking sound with my lips whenever I was thirsty. My right arm was still in plaster, so it burned. Sharon, mummy and David took turns with the nurses to put an ice pack in my hand. This melted quickly. Very quickly.

Soon, the nurse staff would do their rounds. There was Gail, Linda, Siobhan and Teresa. Teresa and Siobhan were a good laugh. Wee Teresa used to tease me while she was changing me, but I'd get her back by breaking wind when she changed my urine bag. I was becoming more like myself with each passing day — at least personality-wise.

A few days later, Margaret removed all the casts except for the one on my right arm, gently snipping them away. Trevor removed the last remaining one.

"No one in my ward should be in pain like that!" He had a big buzz saw to take it off.

A few days later, two doctors came to visit me in the ward. I didn't like them. They smelt like cigarettes and made me feel uncomfortable while they examined my dressings. They examined me as if I wasn't there. They joked while they prodded me. I knew one of them from somewhere. Yes! That's the doctor who wanted to turn off my life-support.

A few days later, I was wrapped up in tin foil because my core temperature had dropped. All the nurses had really concerned looks on their faces. They examined my charts. Then, a few days after that, my trachoma was removed. I surprised Richard Munn by saying hoarsely,

"Where's my *Dune* video, you dirt bag?" Then, a few weeks later, I was introduced to my first wheelchair and then on to the Lagan Valley gym for physiotherapy.

I can't remember much about this first time. I can recall standing and my urine bag filling slowly. I just wanted to get outside. I was in the Lagan Valley Hospital for a long time. Thank God they were all there: staff, friends and family. Without them, I would not be alive to even tell this story.

5mins — Dad contemplating the television Sept 16th 90

My Father, William Fisher, contemplating television, by Jonathan

Chapter Eighteen: My Father

What can I tell you about my father? Only that…

My mummy called him her "Sweet William" in a heartbreaking letter that she wrote to him when he died. I never got to read the end of it because she couldn't finish it. It was too painful for her.

My dad. We used to trample through the autumn woodlands together, my brothers and I, journeying through the thicket and burr with our faithful dog, Titch, in tow. Smoking a cigarette, my dad would blow smoke into the frosty air. He was handsome, with a laugh like no other.

The smells of autumn were on our Wellington boots whilst we marched along with him, kicking brown decaying leaves. Long-dead apple trees with moss covering them, muddy tracks, footprints and pawprints were all left behind like soft memories.

"How much further, Dad?" I would ask.

"Not much further, Jonathan" he would say.

My father. My daddy.

He was a Royal Marine.

I was four years old, and I remember him and me swimming out to sea, him with me on his back.

"How much further, daddy?"

"Not much further, Jonathan," he would say.

Then my grandfather died, and my dad lost his job. My father had worked at various jobs all his life.

I was playing round the tree in the garden in the old house with my brothers. I was twelve. The front window was open and I looked in briefly at my dad, who was sitting in his favourite chair. All seemed normal. But then, I saw he was bright purple. He was choking.

I heard my mummy screaming.

"Oh God! Billy!"

My sister Sharon was on the settee in the living room. I heard a plate smash, and she rushed to his aid. All hell broke loose. I didn't know where to go. I was in turmoil.

An ambulance was called and took my daddy away.

Next thing I knew, I was in aunt Sally's car on my way with my brothers to my uncle Ronnie's house. My cousin Brain was watching the Falklands War. He is called "Brain" on his birth certificate instead of "Brian" because my uncle Ronnie was a bad speller. My aunt Sally said we had the real brains on our side of the family. She always says I am the best-looking Fisher. A wise woman indeed.

What about my Dad? A long wait. What about my Dad? How much longer, Dad? It seemed an eternity, while the Argentinians strike the United Kingdom's task force. The task force hits back en masse in Harrier jump-jets. I'm not in the least bit interested.

Some years later when I am twenty years old, I meet Margaret Thatcher, the Iron Lady, the Prime Minister, in Lisburn and shake her hand. She says to the assembled crowds, in an assertive speech,

"Go back to your homes and work places, knowing that Northern Ireland will firmly remain part of the United Kingdom."

How much longer, Dad? The waiting seemed without end.

And then, finally, he appears with mummy, looking pale. I am so overwhelmed I can't speak. I just look out of the car window on the way home, my face buried against the window. My face was burning with hidden tears. I was so relieved.

He had had a heart attack. He was told to stop smoking and drinking. Soon after, there were no more walks in the woods. A few years later, at Christmas, he refused to do what the doctors recommended him to do.

I heard voices. There was an expectant hush on Christmas Eve. I was excited, and everything was warm and cosy because of mummy's turkey dinner cooking away in the oven. I opened the door. My father was crying and sobbing uncontrollably in the living room. Sharon was hugging him.

I ran upstairs and hid in the hot press, which was a small room beside the bathroom and the upstairs toilet. There is a big hot water tank upstairs, where we carved our initials on the foam inside the hot press. I shut the door with my hands, breathing rapidly.

I waited. Then David found me cowering in fear. It was close to midnight when he found me.

The following Christmas morning when we hurried down to the tree, we hardly spoke to one another. There was such a different atmosphere in the house; things had changed. Then, daddy came downstairs, and it was so awkward. As boys, we were shy and didn't know how to, well, interact. We certainly had hang-ups.

Some years later, our daddy found another job — one that offered cash in hand with one of his mates who worked in double glazing. I think that helped him a bit. He took my brother David fishing in Fermanagh with him. I was more interested in other, err, teenage proclivities.

Five years in High School — Laurelhill High School. The very first day, my form tutor told me I have the build of a woman.

"Excuse me! What did you say?"

His name was "wolf man" Jack Donnelly. He was given that name by other previous pupils and used by another equally hairy pupil, Alan Wilson. Alan started shaving when he was three, I think. He must have come out of the womb like that. More school chums included Richard Black, from Ballymacash Primary School, while some notable others include Philip Millar, Darren Carson, Ivan McGalway, Alan "Paddy" Patrick, Brian McKinley, Colin Moore, Julian Mullins, and Robert Hunter, who were in my various forms. All but a few have drifted away to live their own lives. But, Richard Black, my oldest friend, has always kept in touch, as has Alan Wilson. I drew on Alan's school bag a "Groovy man D.R. and Quinch" from *2000 AD* comic, for which he was eternally grateful. Another guy was Richard "the Dinger" Bell. He was built like a miniature Hercules. He excelled at Sports Day, especially at the shot-put and javelin. Richard always supported the underdogs. He always picked David and me for his basketball team in gym because we were so weedy and thinly built. He thought I was an artistic genius because I managed to forge his history homework for him for Mrs Dodds-Harris. She could tell that Rick didn't do it. It was too good, but she said very little.

Brian McKinley once said,

"Jonathan, you have more brains than anyone else in our class!"

More memorable moments included the infamous history trip featuring toothpaste and me, scarring the girls on the trip for life. But, these things have to be done. Basically, I walked calmly into the girls' dorm while they were all doing their nails. The girls chatted away amongst themselves. They had no idea of what was about to ensue. As I prepared to unleash my epileptic fit on them all, Alan and Richard simultaneously turned out the lights. The screams were heard from Greencastle to Lisburn and beyond.

Then, we all watched John Carpenter's *The Thing* on VHS the following evening. Mrs Dodds-Harris and Mr McCully were not amused.

Once, I dumbed myself down to impress a girl. I was the class clown. I could have gotten straight As in my O-Levels, but I acted the class fool for her. She was a rich girl and, in second year, when my hormones were completely raging way out of control, she asked me in a woodwork class, as she was polishing a bit of wood,

"Would you go out with me?"

I gagged and spluttered and shook my head. I looked downwards to the hell of stupidity that was insecurity.

Her name was Barbara H. and I was smitten.

Then, in forth year, Deborah Mc made her desires known. We were in maths. I was sitting beside Colin Moore in the front row and she at the back. She was the class honey, babe, and sex bomb. She called out to me,

"I want to fuck you hard, Jonathan, and have your babies!"

Colin Moore said to me,

"Well, Jay," he laughed. "She wants to have your children!" He nudged me.

Oh. My. God. Was she serious or delirious?

But, sadly, I was so consumed with unrequited "love" for Barbara H. that I never got to fuck anyone at High School. You never get a second chance with Deborah!

Once, outside the football pitches, I walked into the goal posts whilst looking at Barbara H. rather than looking where I was going. Paddy and Richard Black saw this, as did most of my form. They laughed their balls off. I was a bloody loser in love and romance. Nothing ever changes.

I am ten and back at home in the old house. It's morning, a cold morning with frost on the window-sill of my bedroom. The condensation is making little rivulets down the inside frame. The sparrows are bleedin' chirping outside the window whilst having sex. Down below, I hear the humming of the milk float. Everything else is quiet, save for the clink, clink of the milk bottles being collected by Alan, the milkman. I can't hear the sparrows anymore. Strange. Everything is still in the morning.

I can't hear the sparrows having sex.

I get out of bed to investigate the eerie silence.

I look out the window. Through the blinds I look down to the neighbour's coalbunker. Then I saw a sight to make my skin crawl. It had a face, distorted like a shape from hell. It crouched on the coal-bunker. My skin froze, as did everything in my world. This thing was like a demon gargoyle with a face that was inconceivable. It said one word to me. It turned to look straight into my eyes.

"Peekapeekaboo."

I freaked out. I screamed, "Mummmmmmyyyyyyyy! Daddddddyyyyyyyy!"

There are some things in this world, which cohabit with reality along with us, and I had just seen one. It was real. The Peekaboo monster was coming for me!

My screaming woke the whole house, and quite possibly the whole street. It was real, but when my parents looked out the window at the street below, there was a big, fat nothing.

So, for safety's sake, I crawled into my parents' bed. It was comforting to me to lie in between the two of them. They would guard me against the evil Peekaboo monster forever. There was a feeling of love in that room that I couldn't hope to describe back then. They were lovers, I realise now.

They made sacrifices so that their children could live. I thought they would live forever. But they live through me. The eternal lovers.

But nothing lasts forever.

My dad was diagnosed diabetic. Then he took glaucoma and could hardly see. Before my crisis, I sketched some loving portraits of him. Some of him sitting watching the television, some of him sleeping. Then, one day, we were watching television in the living room and a programme came on about Fathers and Sons. I got emotional and I said,

"Come here, Dad, stand up."

He stood up and said, "What is it, Son?"

And I hugged him hard and said, "I love you, Dad. Don't forget that."

He replied, "That's not us, Son, on the television. We're okay. I know."

Then I took sick.

The crisis and everything that went along with it meant nothing was the same for all of us. After Lagan Valley, I was sent via the Royal to Forster Green Hospital for rehabilitation therapy. I got to go home on occasional weekends and at Christmas. We had one more Christmas as the whole family. 1993.

The following November, things went downhill for my daddy. He took the flu, was sent to the Royal, had massive surgery for his heart and died shortly afterwards.

My dad. My father. My daddy. My mummy's Sweet William.

We cremated him.

That Spring, we went sailing on a yacht that belonged to a friend of my dad's. Uncle Jerry, aunt Sadie, Gordon Davis, the owner of the boat, my sister Heather, her daughter Ella and mummy — all of us were aboard. I was lifted by these big strong men into the boat in my travel wheelchair. At this point, I was still weak from my crisis and felt tremendously sick. But, other than that, it was a perfect sunny day.

The sea gulls were calling. We were somewhere off the coast of Carrickfergus. The engines had stopped.

"How much further, daddy?"

"Not much further, Jonathan."

As my mummy and Heather sprinkled my father's ashes into the sea, my niece, Ella, looked at me with a puzzled expression on her face and said,

"Nanny, why is uncle Jonathan crying?"

She was only four years old.

Mummy just replied, "Because he's sad, Ella, because he's sad," and hugged me.

What can I tell you about my father? Only that I love him.

My Father sleeping, by Jonathan

My Mother.
Tired.

I am fairly happy with
the likeness in this sketch.
However the eyes leave much
to be desired; and ruin the
overall impact.

230

Mummy, by Jonathan

CHAPTER NINETEEN: MUMMY

I am two years-old. My mummy is pushing my brother and me in our pram. My name is Jonathan, and I have curly white blonde hair. My brother is called David, and he cries a lot. He looks like me! I am told these facts by mummy.

Oh no! It's a grey day somewhere. It's called a park. Our mummy is pushing us away from her and bringing us back again, like a game.

"Wheeeeee!" she says!

Our mummy is very pretty. She is blonde, like me, but she wears her hair in a strange way, like a bun we would like to eat. We are at the park with lots of other girls and boys who are busily playing around us, enjoying the roundabouts and the swings! The swings look like fun! I can see a wee girl playing on the swings with her daddy. She has curly hair and they look happy together playing! I spy with my little eyes something beginning with the letter "B!" I can see a birdie in the sky. And a woof-woof making a woofing noise.

I like woof-woofs. They lick our hands when they are sticky with lollipops. They clean our hands! I giggle and laugh when they tickle my hands. We have a big, big, big woof-woof at home; she is called Lady and she lives in our coal-bunker and eats all our coal. She is black, like coal, and she has long ears and a long tongue that laps in her mouth. My daddy built a woof-woof-house for Lady, but she likes the coal-bunker more! She has a long tail that wags and wags a lot. She is funny. We all like her, especially my sisters, Heather and Sharon. My sisters are nice. They push our pram and change our smelly, smelly nappies. I have a push trolley that makes me walk. I love walking!

"Wheeeeee!" says mummy again, pushing us away again.

Where is she? Where has she gone? We look behind us, stretching to look out behind our pram. David starts to squeal. And I start to cry along too.

There you are! Oh, it was just a game! She reappears like, well… I suppose we have to learn how to label things, so we'll just call that one "magic." She reappears like magic, right in front of us! Our magical mother. Our miraculous mummy.

We start fighting in our pram.

I say "Shurrup, David!" but he won't stop. There is a funny man wearing a dog collar walking by us and he tilts his hat to my mum. He is called a Minister, but he looks silly in his collar. Only woof-woofs have collars! He asks mummy our names as he looks into our pram.

"David and Jonathan."

And he says to mummy, "Oh, well named, Ma'am!"

It truly was a miracle how our mother brought her family up to adulthood.

My brother loves his "Go!" It's a wee ball that he throws.

I am growing up! We are three. I have a red scooter that I love to scoot around, up and down the entries of our home in Belfast. We live at three-one-eight Donegall Road in Belfast. We live in the troubles, but I don't see any troubles anywhere! We live beside a big garage.

I remember we share a potty, my brother and I, which is in the living room. Daddy has a study beside the living room where he keeps his fishing magazines and there's a wooden carving of him shooting quacks with his shotgun and his

Jonathan, aged 4

woof-woof Lady is holding a quack-quack in her mouth. My daddy is a hunter. He hunts for fishes and quack-quacks all over the countryside. There is a big piano in this room too, with lots and lots of books, and at Christmas there is a Christmas tree. We have chocolate Santas around it. My cousin Nicky, uncle Jerry and auntie Sadie's daughter, took away the chocolate. I told on her. She is very naughty.

Upstairs, we have a tin bath that mummy pours hot water into. I dip my toes in. I share it with David. We share a bedroom together. It has a fireplace in it. It has a single cigarette butt in the grate. They are yucky. I don't like them.

Upstairs, there is my sisters' bedroom. A big clock chimes every hour, but there is an old oddly shaped clock upstairs too. It is spooky. I don't like it.

Oh, and one day, a bird flew in through the upstairs window! It was a pigeon! I know this because my uncle Roy, who lives in the far away land of Rathcoole, has a large menagerie. I know this word because I watch *Star Trek* with my daddy who loves "science fiction" — more words my daddy taught me. I am smart!

Uncle Roy has a big collection of animals at his home. It's like a zoo. He has a badger, a red fox, and lots of very exotic animals. We know all these big special words because my uncle Jack is very smart. He has a big library in his house, which my sisters like, and he has encyclopaedias, which are given to guide us in our journey through life. He lives with my Auntie Ann. He gave me a book on Astronomy. It's about the night sky! It's a Ladybird book. I like ladybirds too. They are called insects. Some insects are creepy crawlies that "fly" into our house. I really don't like those.

When we visit our uncle's house, daddy drives us in his car. Uncle Roy gave us a gerbil! David squeezes it! We call him "Hammy."

When mummy and daddy go out at night to a place called the Legion, David won't let her out of his sight, so mummy is very wise and smart and she puts her cardigan on my sister's big, big teddy bear.

The following morning, Hammy won't move his wheel. His wee buck-teeth are showing. He won't move and he smells really bad. What's wrong with Hammy, mummy? Mummy says poor Hammy is dead.

"What's 'dead', Mummy?"

She goes on to tell us a little about death. I'm not really interested. I pick my nose absent-mindedly. I pick out of my nose a long trail of mucus. With my finger and thumb I roll it into a ball. I flick it away. I am sure I will find out later about this 'death' thingy. We bury Hammy in the front garden in one of daddy's socks.

We love Airfix toys and Lego and my brother and I fix up and build a big praying mantis and scorpion from Airfix. We fight imaginary battles between the monsters! One day, I built a very, very big pyramid out of Lego. It almost reached to the ceiling!

One morning, I am playing with the kitchen scissors, cutting out a shape, and I pierce my thumb. It's bleeding! I start crying!

"Mummy! Mummy!" I yell. But my mummy (who is very wise) rushes to my aid. She puts a wee bandage on it and tells me there are special soldiers in my blood who, whenever and every time I get a cut or get sick, rush to help me! I stare wide-eyed at my mummy. She tells me the special soldiers are called "antibodies."

"A bit like Uncle David and daddy?" I ask her.

"No," she says. "They are marines! They are the best!"

Mummy soothes me with a nursery rhyme she knows and puts me on her knee, and bounces me up and down to the song.

"Two little boys had two little toys

Each had a wooden horse

Gladly they played each summer's day

Warriors both of course

One little chap then had a mishap

Broke off his horse's head

Wept for his toy then cried with joy

As his young playmate said:

"Did you think I would leave you crying

When there's room on my horse for two

Climb up here Jack and don't be crying

I can go just as fast with two

When we grow up we'll both be soldiers

And our horses will not be toys

And I wonder if we'll remember

When we were two little boys."

She hugs me, and kisses the war wound.

"That's a sad song, mummy."

"You and David are the two little boys," she says.

One hot day, Uncle Dave comes to stay. I like him. During the night of his stay, there is a big, big, electric storm, and a few weeks later there are real soldiers in our house! I am sleeping when they come to lift me and my sisters and brothers to uncle Jerry's house. I hope cousin Nicky won't be there! But she is. I sleep through it all. There are some bad men in balaclavas in our street. The soldiers are there to protect us.

In the morning, the garage beside us isn't there anymore.

I go to nursery school. We go over the wooden railway bridge. We see trains that rattle when we go over with mummy. We can see trolley buses on rails and, in the distance, the nursery school. I play with David and Hughie. At the end of this street, right at the corner, there is a big library and, right in the middle, lives my Granny and Granda Magee. It's a funny name for a street. It's called Utility Street.

My Granny is nice and she always gives us soup. I smelt pepper for the very first time and I sneezed in her soup. Her house is full of very old things. My Granda Magee is a barber. He is called Robert or Bobby. Granny's maiden name is O'Brien. She tells us she has blue blood in her veins because the O'Briens can trace their roots back to the high Kings of Ireland! Ah, go on, Nanny!

My Mummy, Emma Eileen Fisher, by Jonathan

"You think I came up the Lagan in a bubble?" That's one of her expressions, which she regularly teases us with! I like an old music box, which they have. It's in a shape of an old, old car I have never seen before. When we wind it up, it plays a very, very sad melody. It fascinates me and their faces fascinate me, too. They are all wrinkly. At the back of their house is a little house called "the outhouse", which I find really scary. I don't like it one bit, but whenever we go to do wee-wee or poop-poop in there, we have to sit on a wooden plank!

At nursery, we have little beds all laid out in rows in the hall, with girls on one side and boys on the other side. We have naps in the afternoon and we have wee blankets. They are nice and soft and warm. I peek through the blankets to the room. I can see the toy area where the paint-pots are. I love to paint faces and flowers. My teacher says I am gifted. I have never been as safe in my life so far. I love it here, but my mummy wants me to go to the big school in Saint Simon's.

We are four years old and our parents take me to the seaside. We stay in my Granda Fisher's caravan. I meet my other granny. She isn't as nice as my Granny Magee. I go to the seaside to look in the rock pools. I find a crab. It snips me on my thumb, where I cut myself last time. The crab's bad and must be punished! So I pull off its pincers and set it in the rock pool. I realise something: how will it walk? I can walk, but it can't. I feel confused. My face has an odd expression on it. I feel I can imagine I am the crab. It looks at me with its long stalk-like eyes. I feel sad when like I cry. It's like a toothache in the heart. I feel I can put myself into the crab's body. I feel "empathy" for it. "Poor wee thing," I say, and put it softly in a wee pool of salt water with some green stuff called algae.

I must go. My daddy is going to help me learn to swim.

I drop a milk bottle and it smashes on the front doorstep. I was trying to impress mummy so that I can show her I am a big boy who can make his own cornflakes. But I make a mess. I am sorry, mummy. She just frowns for a second, gets a brush and pan and cleans it up. I thought she would shout at me. I feel empathy again.

We all go to a funfair called a circus. Heather and I go on the Ghost Train together, and the Helter Skelter! It's fun! All the rest are too chicken! Wheeeeee! We go up, really, really high up and then race down together.

We go to the zoo — a real one — with my school friends. We sing a song on the school bus!

"We're going to the zoo, zoo zoo, how about you, you, you? You can come too, too, too, we're going to the zoo, zoo, zoo." We are all so happy!

One of our friends goes near a bird called a Toucan. It has a brightly coloured beak. The Toucan bites his nose nearly clean off! It's so funny we laugh very hard.

I like a girl called Tracy. We play trucks and I have a biscuit tin for my trucks, but she puts a dead ladybug in my tin. I look at her. I think she's pretty, but my friends and my brother tease her. And she did put a ladybug in my toy tin. I look back at her and hear my friends calling. I am torn. Tough call. Ummm, sorry, Tracey, it's over between us.

In school, we are sitting around a table. I am sitting at one end. The teacher is sitting at the other. She wears glasses and so I call her Mrs Glasswise. My school friends are all laughing and squabbling and the teacher looks tired. Teachers teach us things so that we can learn new things. I love to learn new skills, so I look round and clap my hands, once, very loudly. My hands sting with the effort. Everyone turns to look at me in silence. Mrs Glasswise says,

"Why, thank you, Jonathan!" She nods at me, bowing slightly.

Then one time I want to wade in the Lagan River! My daddy takes us to Lady Dixon Park where Lady can sniff round other dogs' pooh-pooh bum-bums. I climb trees, run races with David, throw sticks for Lady, and blow dandelion clocks and pick buttercups. Daddy teases me, saying I am "in love", because the buttercups have these stain things called yellow pollen and if you get a stain on your chin, you're "in love."

"I am not in love! I am not!" So I wander off saying, "Stupid daddy!"

I see water! I wonder if I can wade in there like in the rock pools by the seashore! So I roll up my trousers and take off my socks and shoes and wade into the Lagan. Immediately, I realise this isn't a good idea. I start to sink in the mud, and every step I take makes it worse and I go deeper into the soft, soft sticky mud. I am waist-high in the mud. Now, I shout really, really hard.

"Daddy! Help!"

But no one can see me because I'm down an embankment.

I sink further down into the mud.

My screams and yells alert a passer-by and, thankfully, he and daddy arrive just in time to rescue me!

It is early 1977 and daddy takes us to see *Star Wars* at a place called a "cinema", or the "pictures", as my Nanny Magee calls it. It's fantastic! Later, in February, my brothers are watching television and an advert comes on. It's for *2000 AD*! It is Tharg the Mighty! He has come to Earth to give us the gift of thrill power and my whole vocabulary changes over night. This rich lexicon of words: Drokk; Grud; Stomm! I do believe that *2000 AD* transformed my imagination and I was no longer a boy. I was a Terran Earthlet!

It was revolutionary. It fed on my young mind and I loved the stories, including "Judge Dredd," "Invasion 1999," "Harlem Heroes", and my favourite, "Flesh" which is about a company from the future that goes back in time using time machines to harvest Dinosaur flesh! Time machines! Monsters! Lawmen from the future! Basketball players with jet packs! Volgan invaders from Russia! It was all so amazing. Previously, American comics were in the schoolyard, but when we went up the road to our local newsagents, it was jam-packed with the local juveniles, all clamouring to get their hands on Prog One! It had a Space Spinner attached to the issue.

Quite suddenly, I was back in the house, sitting in the middle of the settee, reading "Harlem Heroes", engrossed within the pages, and then my mummy walks into the living room. It's quiet and the television isn't on. She goes and stands by the fireplace and wraps a towel around her hair. She was in the bath. That's all she wore. I look up from my comic briefly and look at her and then very quickly return to *2000 AD*. My eyes stare straight ahead, wide-eyed. It was a real eye-opener and no mistake.

She never said a word, nor did I.

Hey! Where's my scooter gone? I usually park it out the front! Some thieving bad boys have lifted it! I loved that scooter!

Then, one day, I took daddy's gun dog Lady out for a walk up the Donegall Road on a rope. I was the man! This big black Labrador was at least twice my size. But she was getting on, and she was starting to show rage syndrome. That's what it's called, I believe. Anyway, this old tramp went by, and Lady didn't like the look of him. She went for him and bit his arm. I managed to pull her away, shouting "Bad dog! Bad Lady!"

The tramp wanted his piece of flesh so I told him where I lived. Soon, the tramp came round when we were having our dinner — sausages, mash and brown sauce. Lovely. He told my dad his side of the story and then, after some rowing amongst the family, it was decided that Lady would go to a very, very special place called "Doggie Heaven." Funny that. The van that came for poor Lady didn't say that on the side. It said, "Glue Factory." No, I am joking; it said, "Dog Warden."

It was time to change house and we did. In summer 1977, we moved to Lisburn. It was early summer — July. I loved number 38 Rathvarna Gardens. I loved the countryside. There were green fields all around us with barley fields to the south, and to the north there were countless hills and quarries for us to explore.

Then time marched by. Through teenage angst, trials and tribulations, the whole family grew up, earned their diplomas, built lives, and moved on. My sisters got married, had children, and left photographs on my parents' walls. David joined the Royal Navy.

And me? Well, I did a lot of voluntary work after the Tech, met the guys at Outer Limits, joined the Territorial Army, became employed at Bryson House as a trainee graphic designer, met two women, fell in and out of love with them, became employed by Express Litho as a graphic designer and finally died in the arms of my mother.

After my father's death and following my rebirth, my mummy wanted me home so that she could nurse me and she got her wish. She spoiled me and kept me from experiencing real life. She sheltered me in a tiny downstairs bedroom. For close to eight years, I was cooped up in a frustrating, sexless, self-absorbed, cold world wherein I became obsessive and clueless. I was mentally unwell and unfinished. My mind and body were stunted and underdeveloped. I knew I was turning into a vegetable. In front of the fireplace I would sit and the fumes would overpower me. The only social intercourse I had with any people involved the weekly trips out to the local shops in my antiquated wheelchair to buy magazines and papers to read. It was like being back in that pram from all those years ago. The only exercise was standing at the sink or, on a good day, the back gate, with my mummy firmly grabbing onto my right shoulder. I was glad to be alive, standing beside her.

We both looked out at the fields, saying nothing, but we had shared the same heartbeat for six months (David and I were three months premature).

Friends visited. They were having fun, building careers, finding girlfriends, having families of their own. I felt like I was being left behind. Richard Black, Paddy, Richard Munn and the Malones all kept in touch — the old guard.

I love you, mummy. She would preen me and gently do my hair, my beard, wash me, help me to the toilet. I was her baby son again. She would tuck me in at night and say the Lord's Prayer every night, kissing my forehead goodnight for almost a decade.

The toll on her body was appalling. Then, her youngest brother, my Uncle Roy, died of cancer. My Aunt Joan was a lovely lady. She wailed,

"Roy, Roy, my beautiful Roy, sweet Jesus…" His coffin was in the living room as an open casket. Her tears were like floods of biblical proportion. My mummy went to his coffin, as did Heather. Mummy kissed him on his forehead and said, "Goodnight, Son."

When my Uncle Roy was a young boy, he was a celiac. Mum used to tell me about tales from the old house in Utility Street. During the Second World War, my Granda Magee was an ARP Warden. Granny Magee brought up her family — Jack, Emma, Francis, David and Roy. They fought like cat and dog. One time, it was reported that Granny Magee poured a bowl of boiling soup on Granda Magee's head. Uncle Roy needed potassium, or the substance in bananas, to survive. But, during the war, there were no bananas. Anyway, in order to survive and live, he and mummy and Uncle Jack took him to a local slaughterhouse where he was given blood from an ox or cow or a pig. The slaughterhouse guy opened a vein and poured fresh blood into a bowl for him to partake.

"Goodnight, Son", she said to my Uncle Roy. She didn't shed a tear.

Aunt Joan hired a piper to play "Amazing Grace", Uncle Roy's favourite hymn. No one was singing and so I decided to pipe up. I started singing. "Amazing grace, how sweet the sound. I once was lost, but now I la la laaaaa, sweet la aaaaaa!"

I had forgotten the words, but it didn't matter. The rest of the Magee clan joined in. Goodbye, Uncle Roy.

The stress and the post-traumatic events of daddy, Roy and me, all combined in my mother and brought on irritable bowel syndrome. She had to go into hospital for minor surgery. Yeah, where had I heard that one before?

I was so scared. So, after a lot of hot debate in the family, our mother was rushed into hospital. I was deemed incapable of looking after myself, so a care package was set in place by the social worker.

They ripped mummy apart. The surgeons at the hospital took away half her bowel, put in a colostomy bag. Her pain must have been excruciating.

Time passed. Events unfolded. And, mercifully, thank God above, she survived the first operation.

She survived another year with the bag in place. She stopped smoking. We had one last Christmas together. She was getting stronger. So she decided to go in for the reversal to sew her bowel back into place and that was when it all went wrong. The last time I saw mummy alive was in the Lagan Valley Hospital. She was moaning, delirious. I couldn't even hug her, kiss her, and hold her hand, in fear of my wheelchair running over the bed cables. Heather said,

"It doesn't look too good, Jonathan." She told me to go home in my electric pathetic wheelchair.

On the way home, I was the loneliest man on the planet.

The following night, she passed away.

I love you, mummy.

Today is the day of my wonderful mummy's funeral and I am with my David. He is clasping my hand, our hands splayed together. He is a special naval soldier called a Chief Petty Officer. He is wearing his uniform. I love him. He is strong. I like the song mummy sang to us both.

"Two little boys had two little toys

Each had a wooden horse

Gladly they played each summer's day

Warriors both of course

One little chap then had a mishap

Broke off his horse's head

Wept for his toy then cried with joy

As his young playmate said:

'Did you think I would leave you crying

When there's room on my horse for two

Climb up here Jack and don't be crying

I can go just as fast with two

When we grow up we'll both be soldiers

And our horses will not be toys

And I wonder if we'll remember

When we were two little boys.'

I stand up to say the Lord's Prayer. I don't know how I did that, standing up from my wheelchair. I was in floods of tears. There is a Minister called George in our church… I remember:

"We start fighting in our pram.

I say 'Shurrup, David!' but he won't stop. There is a funny man wearing a dog collar walking by us, and he tilts his hat to my mum. He is called a Minister, but he looks silly in his collar. Only woof-woofs have collars! He asks mummy our names as he looks into our pram.

'David and Jonathan.'

And he says to mummy,

'Oh, well named, Ma'am!'"

After the service, the whole family fragmented. Exploded. Some nasty family members complete with their own schemes and plans within plans, which I could not see, left me in the lurch. They know exactly who they are and what they did and did not do. The "spider", the elder "brother", a shadow creature of a man, who will remain forever nameless in this story, weaved his web so well.

So, when mummy died, I was forced out onto the street, to leave my home in which I grew up and paid for, by the machinations of a scheming, evil, mad man. Whereas David loved me and cared deeply for my welfare, the "spider" hated me all my life, with sibling jealousy and rivalry escalating to the point where I hit him and drew blood. I am not proud of what I did. He held a grudge all those years, even before I took the crisis, but as a form of revenge he threatened and tortured me psychologically, and physically, his own disabled brother. He admitted once in front of David and me saying,

"I didn't give a damn when Jonathan got sick!" I draw a veil over these events. If I did not, I would go completely cuckoo. I was forced to move into a smelly, roach-infested old people's nursing home. I was there for close to six months. I was mentally unwell, crazy and I got infections galore in that hole. And then…

"Long years had passed, war came so fast.

Bravely they marched away.

Cannon roared loud, and in the mad crowd

Wounded and dying lay.

Up goes a shout, a horse dashes out

Out from the ranks so blue

Gallops away to where Joe lay.

Then came a voice he knew:

Did you think I would leave you dying

When there's room on my horse for two?

Climb up here, Joe, we'll soon be flying.

I can go just as fast with two.

Did you say, Joe, I'm all a-tremble.

Perhaps it's the battle's noise.

But I think it's that I remember

When we were two little boys.'"

("Two Little Boys" song lyrics by Rolf Harris)

David came and took me out of that place. He found me a house of my own, a place to call my home.

David and Jonathan

Jonathan, aged 21. Self-portrait

CHAPTER TWENTY: VOLUNTEERING

Early 1990.

"She is, umm, black," said Mandy, whispering.

"Umm, so?" was my reply.

Mandy Sheerluck was the co-coordinator for Voluntarily Served Lisburn, a prim and proper youngish woman for the said service. She was a pain in the rectum to work with, always looking over my shoulder. I think she might have fancied me. But anyway, the black person in question, looking up at us, was Martha Washington from the comic book series *Give Me Liberty*, published by Dark Horse Comics, that I loved. *[Jay Note: Give Me Liberty was created by Frank Miller and Dave Gibbons.]* I had taken it upon myself to build, paint and design a fraggin' huge float for the Lord Mayor's parade that year. It was to be VSL's centre-piece for the parade.

I loved *Give Me Liberty*. When Martha comes home from the Amazon War to see her "Mom", that single word did it for me, so much so I went home that evening and gave my own sweet mom a big hug.

I had wanted to give something back to the community, as I had been unemployed for so long. Back then, Lisburn could have been twinned with Dixieland in the Deep South, complete with duelling banjos and all that other racist, bigoted malarkey. Well, not much has changed, to tell you the truth, although it has got better…

My slogan was to be: "Break Down Barriers", and so I copied Martha, running in a marathon, breaking red tape. It could have been like Michelangelo's Sistine Chapel. That was my inspired vision.

So there we were, looking up at this big sketch that I had done. There were dreadlocks in Martha's hair to make it less like a graphic novel. We were in the big storage area above VSL.

I never thought anything more about her skin colour. My cousin on my dad's side of the family is black. Cousin Nicky is a really nice guy. Besides, two characters in our favourite television shows, while we were growing up, were black! Huggy Bear from *Starsky and Hutch* and Lieutenant Uhura from *Star Trek*. Huggy was the man and Uhura was one sexy foxy mama!

Mandy folded her arms and pursed her lips and said,

"It's hard to say this, Jonathan, but it's not really what I was thinking. I mean, she's a runner…"

She was obviously going to say something else.

"Mandy, look, it will be fine," I said sharply to her. "So what do you want on the other side of the float? I could do the VSL logo on the opposite side, a really big, big one? What do you think?"

She paused to reconsider. "No, we need the runner on both sides because…." ya da ya da blah blah blah whaa whah… Like Charlie Brown's teacher, I stared at her. Time slowed down immeasurably when she said "No". Maybe the paint fumes were getting to me. My perception was going white. I was fading out, losing focus. I stared at her.

I have learnt never to argue with a woman, whenever her mind's made up.

"Fine, you'll get your fraggin' feckin' bastard float!" I muttered under my breath.

"What did you say, Jonathan?" she took a step closer.

"Oh, nothing."

She returned my stare, examining me briefly. And then she looked at me, peered over my shoulder and went down the stairs, clicking her high heels behind her like some cloven-hoofed witch.

"Crom! Why?" I shouted at the empty hall, clenching my fists. I went down on my hands and feet in front of the float, curling into a ball. I closed my eyes, squeezed them tight. What does not kill us makes us stronger…

I opened one eye and peeked up at it. This was big. The biggest painting I ever did and it was entirely out of my artistic control. Therefore, I absolutely hated it. And so I enlisted the aid of Paul and Robert Malone to aid me in this quest.

"Guys!" I wailed. "You've got to help me! Infamy! Infamy! They've all got it in for me!"

I was up to my neck in paint-pots, red vinyl deluxe, and brown paint. My hands were covered in stains and I was getting high on paint fumes.

Paul said in a sympathetic tone,

"Jay, if you want, I could bring you a facemask and my airbrush?"

Robert added, "You want some photographs for your portfolio, Jay mate?"

"Thanks, guys." I picked up a huge two-by-four plank and just as I was about to smack the float, I paused for a photo opportunity. Then…

Thawck! Thawck! Thawck! I vented my rage on the float.

The guys were on the floor now, literally doubled over with laughter.

It sucked the life out of me for at least a month. It was like an alien chest-burster. I sweated blood and tears into that damn thing, and then came the day for the Lord Mayor's parade.

I was so embarrassed. Mandy Sheerluck had roped some poor suckers in from the disabled school whom I took swimming in my remit as a voluntary worker. They were great kids. Some had mental problems, some had Down's Syndrome.

They did not deserve to be paraded around Lisburn like that.

It was raining hard. One big guy was waving at the crowds. No one waved back but me. I think the sight of a black woman running surrounded by a group of disabled kids was a bit too much for Dixieland Lisburn.

Somewhere, I heard a banjo playing.

This sign hung in the car park of VSL, Lisburn. Hand-painted by Jonathan

Jonathan, aged 21. Self-portrait in oils

CHAPTER TWENTY-ONE: EACH DAY IS LIKE VALENTINE'S DAY

Her name was Joyce Andes. She was a cousin of the Death Bringer, Paul Andrews and, well, I wanted to make her acquaintance — and other things besides.

Going back in time to the previous summer, Ellen was the first girl I had ever kissed. We met in Thompson House while I was doing some voluntary work, feeding some of the elderly folk in the home. All good experience for my CV, as Mandy Sheerluck said.

I used to do little errands for the old folk: trimming moustaches and taking them on trips around the home in their push wheelchairs and outside whenever the weather was suitable. I even helped hold an old geezer's cigarette whilst he took a drag from it. There was this young man with a degrading condition. He was called Kevin. He had been in the Royal Navy — past tense. The poor guy was shaking and slobbering as he sneezed in his wheelchair. I got a big whack of gauze and blew his nose for him. The nurses were having a smoke break. Poor Kevin, he died in that place. He just wasted away.

Anyway, Ellen was seventeen at the time and I was nineteen. She was wearing a flowery blouse that revealed her ample charms. She clocked me, loaded, locked and fired. She introduced herself and shook my hand. She looked like a young Julia Roberts, and I was completely blown away. She wanted to be a volunteer as well. I showed her the ropes, so to speak.

Our first kiss was her first kiss too. It was outside her nana's house on Benson Drive. The air was warm and it was late. We paused. She was wearing a sun hat, but the sun had gone out some time ago. We had walked hand in hand through Lisburn.

She turned and smiled, a tiny smile, and then there was another pause. It was like two magnets drawing closer, closer and closer until, finally, I closed my eyes and then it was real. I was a member of the human race. Another human being had touched my lips, softly. Moistly, we embraced, holding each other's bodies, blood coursing throughout.

So this is what they call love.

But there are many different kinds of love.

We were too young and foolish to understand back then. After the Mourne mountain adventure, Ellen went and did a very foolish thing. She went to the Ulster Starz's offices and, after we had specifically asked for no publicity, she decided to tell the reporter guy all about everything, and a photographer went to her nana's house. I, however, showed them both the door and politely told them to "frag off." Ellen was livid with me, but we started fooling around and I chased her upstairs.

Coyly, she said,

"Jonathan, this isn't fair," as I kissed her body. Deeply I kissed her, but she just lay there half naked on her bed. She did not reciprocate. She looked at me; I knew that she wanted me to make love to her.

I was hard and erect.

Submissively, she gestured, throwing her long brown hair to one side. We were both virgins. I came in my trousers, a sweet warming sensation, but we did not have sex. I did not want to. I asked myself why. She had an amazing body, in all blooming directions.

A week later, I was in our friendly neighbourhood comic store and Paul was the one who was livid with me.

"Jay," he said angrily, showing me the front page of the Ulster Starz, smacking it on the desktop. "What the hell is this?"

It was Ellen. She still wanted her fifteen minutes of fame. There she was, posing bold as brass on the front page, her shoes, her wee rucksack, a map of the Mournes and a fraggin' compass all strewn across the front lawn. Inside was her story of how we rescued the two school kids.

My face went purple. "Excuse me, Paul," I said softly. I pulled my bike from the back room. "I will deal with this."

I pedalled hard and furiously to her nana's house. And, as was to be expected, we had a massive row, although it resulted in more heavy petting. A few weeks later, she gave me the cold shoulder.

"Ellen, what's wrong?"

She looked away from me as we walked through Lisburn. She took her hand away from mine. She mumbled something.

"I want to get on with my career, Jonathan."

I pulled her shoulder where her handbag strap was, but she pulled it away from me, shoving me to one side.

I was in tears. "Ellen, I love you. Don't you love me?"

There are many kinds of love.

She just shrugged me off and walked away from me.

I stood there for a while, tears streaming from my face.

Years later, however, I am a different person, a cripple in a wheelchair. I am twenty-three years old. I've just come back from physiotherapy. I am weak in body and in spirit. My father has passed away and we just buried him at sea. I am in Forster Green Hospital, and I am surrounded by all these old men in wheelchairs, some with MS and various other ailments. All broken men, with broken lives with broken dreams, in broken wheelchairs.

I am not broken.

I hate it here. I hate the world. I long to get out and walk. The therapists are *meant* to be rehabilitating me. In speech therapy, a girl called Gillian has me writing on a BBC micro. Just one sentence: "My name is Jonathan." The effort completely tires me out and reading is very difficult. I read a paragraph from one of my favourite authors, Harry Harrison, *Deathworld*. I stumble and stammer on the piece like when I was a child. In physiotherapy, Carol, Avril and Sandra are teaching my muscles to waken up and to walk. In Occupational Therapy, a man called Wilnor is teaching me to pee in a bottle. I use a horrible device strapped to my leg called a convene. It is a rubber bag, which is attached to my wing wang doodle and leg, because I have no bladder control yet.

I am also taught to wash and clean myself. I can barely manage with my left hand. The toilets and the bathroom are archaic. Wilnor and Mum start teaching me to write with a pencil and encourage me to paint. It is so tiring and difficult because I was originally right-handed. The results are primitive, but nevertheless intriguing.

I was sent to Dublin for a brain scan, but my consultant Viktor and my mum won't let me see it. I am allowed to view it only briefly. Annoyingly, no one seems to have a goal for me to achieve and I wonder why this is. My thoughts are horrible and disgusting and dark. The nurses are pathetic. I don't like the way they handle me or wash me, like they don't care.

No one cares.

Only one person cares — my mum, who is very wise.

Mum says, "You've a visitor, Jonathan."

It was Ellen. "Hello, Jonathan." She gave me that wee timid smile of hers. Her hands were behind her back and she stood standing beside Mum.

I could not face her. I pulled the curtains across in my ward. Well, I tried to, but I was too weak. I was in tears. I could not face her. I was embarrassed and I didn't want her to see me this way. I wanted her to remember me the way I was before.

We would have walked through summer woodlands, chewing grass, kissing and holding hands.

There is a poem I love by Thomas Hardy. It is called "After a Journey":

"Soon you will have, dear, to vanish from me,

For the stars close their shutters and the dawn whitens hazily.

Trust me, I mind not, though Life lours,

The bringing of me here; nay, bring me here again!

I am just the same as when

Our days were a joy, and our paths through flowers."

I am just the same.

So, the irony of it all is that, in the same way as the people I helped, I ended up in a wheelchair too.

Great. Yeah, irony just loves me.

And yes, there are most certainly many kinds of love.

I asked Mum to close the curtains and to ask Ellen to leave. Because I worked in that old folks' home, my stubborn male pride kicked in and I just couldn't accept it. I just couldn't. I was pathetic and, to make matters worse, I felt awful both for her and for myself and for what could have been between us.

How the mighty are fallen.

Meanwhile, in the space between lovers, back at Outer Limits, Joyce Andes had the most amazing grey blue eyes and looked a little like Annie Lennox. She worked in an estate agent's in Lisburn and she passed by the shop a few times. I was reading when she looked in and our eyes met. The next time it happened, I waved at her, flashing my grin and she waved back.

Paul Andrews and I were playing chess. He said,

"I know her, Johnny, she's my thecond cousith."

"Oh, really? She's a honey! Where does she work, Paul?" I raised my eyebrows (and that wasn't the only thing I raised).

So, Paul Andrews gave me some info on Joyce. It was coming close to Saint Valentine's Day and so I decided to make my move. I bought a single red rose from Ronnie Lamont's fruit emporium and a card on which I wrote:

"Ten wasted moments lying on my bed,

Subliminal thoughts and memories boring though my head,

All the time that life could have and bring,

And nothing fills it in,

Throwing hope and reason to this deadly sin.

Ten wasted moments,

Painting life's soul mauve,

Waiting through these centuries

For the thing that thing they call

True love."

Whoa, deep. Anyway, I put my phone number at the end and signed it with a flourish. I had balls of the finest steel back then, and the testosterone of pure Adamantium. *[Jay Note: the metal Adamantium is at the core of Wolverine, the only Marvel comic character I respect, because of his uncanny resemblance to Glenn Danzig, 'nuff said!]* My heart was pounding as I opened the door. The fair maiden Joyce was sitting at her desk inside the estate agent's office and she was on the phone. I went down on one knee and presented her with the card and rose. She was totally shocked, hugging the phone to her chest, open-mouthed, with a look of surprise and bewilderment in her beautiful eyes.

I was wearing my green polo neck jumper and my beard was trimmed for the occasion. Truly, I was a sexy devil, and then some. I am a man of no great wealth, but great taste. I stood up and introduced myself. I shook her hand.

"Hello, my name is Jonathan, Joyce. I am very glad to meet you at last. Ummm, this is for you." I gestured to the card.

"I won't keep you from your work, and well," I kissed her hand. "Happy Valentine's Day."

There was a round of applause and a cheer from her co-workers and they all stood up as I turned and left.

If I smoked, I would have lit up a cigar and said,

"Ah Yorick…" But, I did the next best thing. I got that week's *2000 AD* from Outer Limits and sat and read it with a big grin on my face. The two Pauls thought I was a sex god. And, yes, they were right. The following evening, Joyce telephoned me at home.

Unfortunately, our conversation was a bit awkward. She was a little reticent, but she did say that that was the most romantic gesture anyone had ever done for her. I think she had a boyfriend.

We agreed to meet at the swimming pool and we went for a swim. I was such an adrenaline junkie. However, I think I blew it totally. Picture this, dear reader.

It was a typical Saturday in the comic shop and we were just lounging around and reading comics, drinking tea and coffee, when Joyce suddenly walked by the window, ignoring me. I felt a trembling in the force, or my pants?

I shouted, "Paul! Paul! Guitar, guitar!"

Paul looked confused and looked at me and said "What?"

I snapped my fingers as quick as a flash and I yanked Paul's guitar from his mighty hands and belted down Bridge Street at warp factor 9, with the shops on the street looking on. I tore past Joyce and skidded to a halt in front of her and dropped to one knee.

And so the serenading began. I played a few chords of Chris Isaak's "Wicked Game." Well, that was me blown out totally.

"Yeah, you think?" Paul shook his head and laughed. "Crash and burn, Fisher. Crash and burn."

Still life of cloth on table, by Jonathan

CHAPTER TWENTY-TWO: LOGZILLA

Before we begin, dear reader, I should state that the title of this chapter was suggested by none other than the Munnisher, Richard Munn.

Now, let me tell you. I know what child birth is like.

"Hey, it's Mulligan's birthday this morning! Pass it on!"

It was Julian Mulligan's birthday at Laurelhill High School.

"Oh, really?" I said. "What are we going to give him for his birthday?" I asked my classmates. We were in the fourth year. "Roasties, flushies or the bumps?" His birthday was one day after Valentine's Day.

Roasties were usually handed out to first year students, which would involve the "victim" being tortured on the hot radiators that lined the corridors, using the victim's testicles as a friction break. Nice.

Flushing, as the name suggests, involved the Birthday Boy being forced to drink toilet water whilst encrusted faeces washed his hair. Lovely. However I hasten to add this was an urban myth. No one actually did this…but who knows what really went on in the boys' toilets at Laurellhill?

Julian was the class genius. He looked pale and pasty-faced and had shocking brown curly hair, like a goat. He had deep intelligent blue eyes and a stubby nose, and he always wore his fleece-lined jacket and so we named him Sheepy Mulligan. His complexion was a result of playing Elite, the space-trading game on a variety of home computers: BBC micros, Spectrums, and Atari ST. Any computer problem? Go to Mulligan!

This guy was so intelligent he almost wiped out the entire network of BBC B computers in the school, making what appeared to us a crude computer virus, but in fact Mulligan accidentally modified the system administrator's login script so that it just messed up his screen and made it look like the whole network was knackered. All completely innocent. It locked up the old Apple II computer that was slaved into all the BBC B micros. The teacher was furious with him!

"Fix it, Julian!" he roared.

This evil genius was also our bitch.

The computer lab was on C floor and that's where we started. We opted for the bumps. Good choice.

Phillip Millbug and Ivan Tinswald were the class's big fellas. Jules put his school bag down and shrugged at me. He looked at me curiously and said,

"What's up, Jay?"

With a sincere look on my face, I replied, wide-eyed and innocent, with,

"Why, Julian, your shoe lace is untied!"

As he bent down to look, I gave my classmates the nod and they started hoisting Julian into the air.

"You bastards! Get the fucking hell off me!"

We all took a limb each and proceeded to go all along the C floor at full pelt, singing,

"Happy Birthday to you! Happy Birthday to you, dear Julian, happy birthday to you!"

He thrashed and squirmed. He was strong — very strong, in fact. But not strong enough.

It was like a mosh pit where you staged into a crowd!

"Hey! You boys, put him down!" roared the wolf man.

Jack Donnelly had heard the racket. He had come out of his lair to investigate the commotion.

Immediately we put Julian down, gently…

Julian and I became good friends. During one summer, I had him over for mummy's homemade lasagne and we played on his Atari ST upstairs in my bedroom. During the following summers, we parted for a while. He went to University of Ulster at Coleraine to study Computer Science. He was the first ever listener of the John Fisher Radio Show outside Lisburn. He listened in Moira, the mud-hole. That's where he lived. I would phone him up every Tuesday night at five pm so that he could tune in to us.

I would meet him every Friday when he got off the train after the comic shop closed. He would wait for his mum outside the bus station behind Greanz food emporium. It is noteworthy to state that Mrs Mulligan had the hots for Captain Kirk, the Shatnermeister himself. We would sit and chat over tea, scones and other delicacies in the Greanz coffee dock. Every week we'd do the same thing, for six months or so.

We sat for ages. I would show him my latest sketches and he would talk about the latest software languages. We were both young men with a lot of promise and a great many ideas.

Our conversations were wide, varied and always stimulating. You see, our friendship was similar to the characters in *Deep Space 9*. I was like Garak, the sophisticated, debonair assassin and Jules was the intelligent, handsome Julian Bashir. *[Jay Note: Andrew Robinson played both Scorpio in the movie Dirty Harry and Garak in the television series Star Trek: Deep Space 9.]*

It is July, about three months after I had died. I had just celebrated my twenty-second birthday. Whoopie-fecking-doo. I am in Lagan Valley hospital. My body is starting to heal — slowly. My trachea is still in but I can speak with a rasp. One of the physiotherapists has just sucked my lungs out with the suction machine next to me. I am lying on an ancient hospital bed with my legs, right to my ankles, entombed in plaster. My right arm is the same, but my left is free. Both my hands are full of wires, which the doctors and nurses use to pump a concoction of drugs into me from a drip that hangs above my bed.

For my birthday, I was allowed a fry-up: sausages, bacon, eggs and a little brown sauce. I was spoon-fed by Siobhan, a young nurse with big brown eyes and brown tanned skin. I say this is degrading for me, and she nods her head in agreement and replies,

"Mmmm. I am sure it is, Jonathan." She wipes my mouth gently with some blue wipes, leaving a pile of them for the other nurses and gives me a drink from a feeding cup with a straw in it. I relish it as if it were my last meal.

Some birthday that was. It was hard for me to take all in. After the party in my back garden the previous year, where the Astrozombies rocked the neighbourhood, my life is unrecognisable. The nurses propped up my pillow and I stared out the window, looking vacantly towards the green fields of Lisburn, yearning just to live and run and cycle again. It was getting late and the nurses were about to change their shifts for the evening. I was just about to rest my eyes.

All the other visitors had left and then I heard a familiar voice saying,

"What's up, Jay?" he looked at me curiously.

I smiled.

He shrugged at me.

It was my old friend Julian.

"Julian, come and sit beside me," I gestured to a seat. It was an old school-type seat, taken from the ward. "I'm sorry I can't sit up to greet you, my old friend, or do anything more, to tell you the truth, man! How are you?" We clasped hands.

There was a tear in his eye. "I heard what happened, Jay. I am so sorry, man." He bowed his head and looked away. "If there's anything I can do for you, name it!" He composed himself and looked at me and grinned. He squeezed my hand tighter.

"Thanks Jules, I love ya, man!"

"I love you too, Jay! Got you a card. It's not much, but I think you'll like it!" He opened it for me, saying, "My sister Wanda is in Brazil and she sent me this carnival card… Topless dancers!"

I laughed as hard as I could.

We sat around for a while, talking about old times, laughing and joking. Then I felt something stirring. I had no idea what was happening, or what was about to happen. I felt a cramp. Now I was the one who thrashed and squirmed.

"Jules, help me!" I pleaded.

"Jay, what's wrong? Should I get a nurse?"

"Noooo!" I squeezed his hand hard, digging my fingernails deep into his hand. "No time! They're too busy at this time of night doing their rounds!" I shut my eyes tight from the pain. "I think I am having a crap!"

Then it came. The tremors first, then *logzilla*.

"Jules, get those wipes on the table. Please hurry!" I squeezed.

My legs were apart, waiting to give birth to this monster crap. Jules dutifully complied. He had no other choice. We were both laughing and crying at the same time as he wiped.

"Jay, I think I'm gonna faint!" He gagged at the sight of Logzilla coming towards him at full steam ahead! Boom! Boom! And the smell! The stench in my ward was unbelievable. It came and it came. And it came and it came, and it still came and it continued.

My bowels had not moved for about three months. Not to my knowledge, thanks to the coma.

Without any sort of boast or exaggeration, my excrement was two feet long. It — was — this — big!

One of the night staff appeared at the door. They shouted for assistance. They opened a window and started cleaning up the mess. They said to Julian,

"We'll take over now. You want a job here as a nurse?" they joked. They told Julian to go and wash his hands and wait for me as they closed the curtains for privacy.

The nurses cleaned my backside. It was all very degrading to subject myself to this treatment, and for Julian as well. I apologised to Jules when he returned, looking extra pale.

"Man, you were a real friend back there. That was above and beyond the call of duty, Jules! I love ya, man!" I said out of breath.

"That's okay, Jay, you would do the same for me." He looked traumatised.

"Will you come back to see me tomorrow, Julian?"

"Sure, Jay, I will!" He walked out the door shaking.

Sadly, I never saw Julian Mulligan after that night. A friend of a friend told me he probably went to Brazil to see his sister, before emigrating to the USA. Poor guy. I must have melted his brain with post-traumatic stress disorder, with a little help from Logzilla, the monster turd.

That night ranks as the lowest, most shameful moment of my entire life.

Since that day, I look forward to every bowel movement with great anticipation.

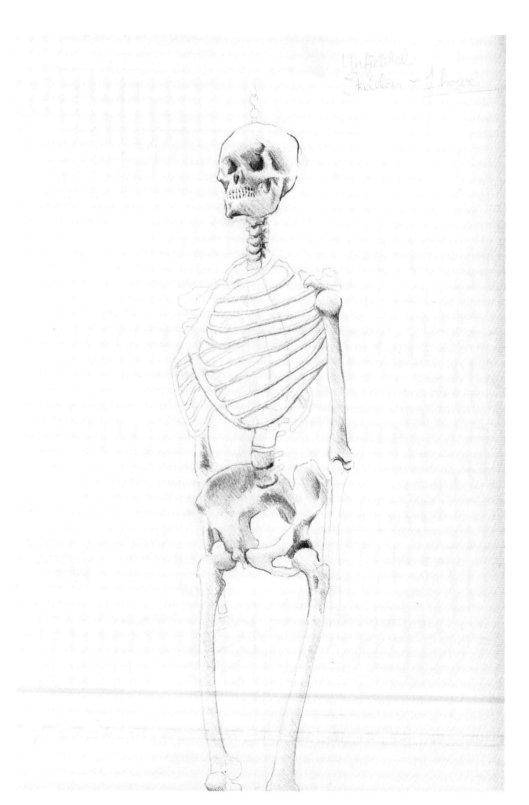

Bones the Skeleton, by Jonathan

CHAPTER TWENTY-THREE: THE GHOST OF HALLOWE'EN TOWN

Walking again. I want to walk. Since the day I died and most of my brain was wiped out by this condition, I have wanted to walk. In the past, how many years it's been, I have been struggling to get on my feet. There have been many doctors, physiotherapists and my own family, that have been either very helpful, or detrimental to my progress in varying degrees. Does that mean I am selfish and bitter? At times, yes. Does that mean I am frustrated and discouraged? I am a human being with rights to determine my own destiny. I fear the future at times, and embrace it at other times. Human beings are very flawed creatures and I am very human. Destiny is a place you want to be in your life. Rights? There is no right or wrong, only points of perspective.

It's only natural to want more and to do more than merely survive. If that makes me a cold, calculating bastard in other people's eyes, then I am. I have sacrificed lovers and relationships to get what I want out of life. But haven't we all?

I have a weakened right side and I tend to compensate with my left. My balance is fornicated, meaning it is F.U.C.K.ED. But I can step now in physiotherapy in my bare feet, in the parallel bars. It is very hard work; only a couple of metres.

A few Christmases back, I stepped over seventeen metres with help from my therapists out of the gym in the day centre I attend. They're amazing people in there. The Rowan Centre to give the place its title. I went swimming. In the local pool, I walked with a therapist at each side, both holding onto my hands to guide me. I walked twenty-one metres.

I also went horse riding. I love horses. I won "Disabled Rider of the Year" for Northern Ireland in 2006/7. During that year I attended a disabled school in Glenavy. My horse was named Sox. I had three helpers, all volunteers. They would assist me at each side and one led my horse. They had a big mechanical swing inside the enclosure to assist the rider on to the horse, from wheelchair to horse. It was exhilarating, and liberating. The rhythm of the horse helps trunk control, stability and stamina. A few times we were led out of the enclosure, into the wild blue yonder! These were on very sunny warm days. Yee haa! "Get those doggies rollin, Rawhide!" *[Jay Note: Rawhide, as previously mentioned in this memoir, is a cowboy adventure series from the early '50s. Whip crack away!]*

Anyway.

I have piloted a glider. I have known briefly what a bird knows. How it soars and flies through the air currents…

One day in October, some lucky clients at the Rowan Centre went up north to The Ulster Gliding Club.

Like Don Quixote, we passed windmills on the horizon as we journeyed through County Antrim. Shortly after 1100 hours we arrived at the airfield where the action was about to unfold. We all received a very warm welcome at the clubhouse and were introduced to Jay Nethercott, our pilot for the day's events, and to Mervyn and Alan, his co-workers. Inside the clubhouse was a breakfast bar, where we had lunch a bit later, a small WC, three round tables, a TV, a computer and fax machine and a very nice painting of a glider. I glanced at the visitors' book, which had entries as far back as the early '80s from people all over the world, all praising the club and those daring men in their flying machines!

I have honestly dreamed of flying all my life. I'm an astronomer and a big science fiction fan that has piloted starships through flight simulators on my computer. I have earned my wings on Elite, the space trading game, I have battled Klingon warships in the inky void that is the vacuum of space, the final frontier, but that is nothing compared to the sheer exhilaration of gliding!

Having been strapped in the glider very firmly with a safety harness, I was towed to the landing strip. Inside, I could see an instrument panel with some dials and other equipment in front and a joystick plumped right smack bang in the middle and, on the left hand side, a small window. Jay climbed in behind me and gave me a quick run-down of the controls. So, we were then connected to the "tug" — the aeroplane — and this had an engine. We were gradually pulled into the air!

It was incredible! The sensation of take-off was quite unparalleled to anything I have experienced in my life. Now I know what it's like to be a bird, an eagle in flight. Then, when we were at the right height, we were released!

Jay took us over the cloud cover and into the sun in the west. I was reminded briefly of the old Greek legend of Daedalus and Icarus. But enough of the history lesson. We soared above the clouds into the air thermals that were being generated from the sun-heated ground below. At this stage, Jay gave me the controls.

Controlling the glider was an experience. To put it simply, another environment to be conquered by the mind. I recalled a passage I have learned off by heart from my favourite novel, *Dune*:

"I must not fear. Fear is the mind-killer. Fear is the little-death that brings total obliteration. I will face my fear. I will permit it to pass over me and through me. And when it has gone past I will turn the inner eye to see its path. Where the fear has gone there will be nothing. Only I will remain."

Focus, breathe…

We dipped and swooped over the clouds, accelerating downwards, slowing down as we pulled up. Banking from side to side, I could see below us the headland cliff formation and the trout river. I asked Jay the name of the town in front of us.

"That's Limavady, Jonathan and, on your right as you look down is Lough Foyle."

Downwards as we swooped I could see the patchwork quilt of fields, with sheep and cows, some running from the shadows of our gliders. The countryside was stunning from the air.

All too soon, Jay resumed flight control. He skilfully did a turnabout towards the landing field. He took us out towards the bay. The sea glittered in the sunshine. He landed with the utmost care and precision and, safely down, I thanked him with a firm handclasp.

Quoting "The Impossible Dream" ("The Quest") by Mitch Leigh and Joe Darion:

"To dream the impossible dream...

To reach the unreachable star...

This is my quest, to follow that star,

No matter how hopeless, no matter how far..."

Dreams do come true.

My progress has always been slow, but now I have progressed to a rollator. It's exactly like the push trolley that I had, when learning to walk as a child.

I did some research online and found a project called Hybrid Assistive Limb (HAL for short) and, thanks to my consultant, I got in contact with the professor in Japan. I have been in monthly contact with a few of the professor's assistants.

276

Professor Sankai is a science fiction aficionado, calling his device after the computer in Stanley Kubrick's "2001: A Space Odyssey", written by the legendary Arthur C. Clarke. Basically, HAL is a Cybernetic device, which, in theory, could help me to regain the strength to walk again.

I can touch people's hearts, and destroy them with words. Words are the only things that I have now. Words will be all that's left of us when we are gone. People will say, "Do you remember such and such or so and so?" Words are the only remains of my parents for all the work they did to bring me up. Some of my words and memories are lost to brain damage, the rest I have tried to recall to the best of my ability in this narrative. Words are weapons of mass deception, corruption and conception. So what if the parts of my brain don't function correctly yet? It is my life and I will live it to full — until the day I die.

That's why I call Lisburn "Hallowe'en Town." Why "Hallowe'en Town," I hear you ask? Well, I could hardly call it "That's your Lot, Salem" as my mother would have said jokingly, or a vengeful lawsuit might ensue. And, secondly, at any given time of year, you will find at least one undead creature roaming through the streets and spires. I will tell you, the whole of the Bow Street's unholy mall is rife with zombies, ghouls, spectres and other such beings from the seventh level of Hades.

They still come out at night, with the more adventurous ones emerging out from the twilight to infest the daylight. Some call them "spideys", "chavs", or "hoodies" — take your pick. The others — the more dangerous kind — are called "millies". These are the brides of Beelzebub, evil cockroaches of doom. Nothing really changes here. Life has come full circle. Lisburn has saved my sweet ass on more than one occasion. We have developed a symbiotic relationship.

This has been my story. Just one of many I wish to tell you, my dear reader...

In my dreams, I am still that precocious nineteen-year-old man. An "uncouth youth," as my father would say.

"Do you know that, son?" he asked me. "Ahh, yes! Happiness is dog-shaped." Beside me there is a tan-coloured Jack Russell dog curled in a blanket snoring. Her name is Titch, and my name is Jonathan Fisher. The ghost and the dark night of Hallowe'en Town.

"Pleased to meet you!"

I hope you feel the same…

Wine Glass, by Jonathan

CHAPTER TWENTY-FOUR: AUGUST ALWAYS

August was her name. Autumn was his.

The two friends sat in the park. They shared two Cornish pasties together. The crumbs went everywhere. She wore a light-red jumper and a necklace with stars on it, which accentuated the golden colour of her red hair. The necklace was a gift from him.

It was a beautiful summer's day at the end of May when they decided to go their own separate ways. They didn't mind the crumbs. Their hearts were breaking.

She brushed him down. They shared a bottle of mineral water together.

August played on the park swing. Back and forth she went and to and fro, like a pendulum. Her golden-red hair shone in the sunlight. He wished with all his heart that he could have joined her, but he was disabled from a brain injury, and this had condemned him to a wheelchair, with the passing of time — the movement of the clock's hands and the leafing of the calendar — as the only way of surpassing the torture.

He felt so impotent. If only he could have joined her. She was so alive.

She treated him like an equal and, quite simply, he couldn't accept that. He felt that he was superior to everyone, but he had changed. She had shown him he was a human being. She had brought out his humanity. She had shown him her world and what it means to be human, with all the majesty and failings, like everyone had.

They were both in tears. She said,

"My love, you're not okay? I'm sure you're not!" She came off the swing to comfort him. She wondered, "You know there must be something wrong in my head, too, otherwise I wouldn't be here with you." She tutted for the first and only time they had known each other. She held him and kissed him gently on his lips.

"Ach, sweetheart," she said softly. "Come here!" She hugged him hard.

He was dumbfounded. He had nothing to say. They were lovers for a year or so, but he had lied about stupid insignificant things and this had torn them apart.

"Promise me something," she said. "Promise me you'll be a good friend to me always?"

He nodded his head in agreement, and said, "Yes."

He loved the tiny things about her: the way she snored late at night when they were together; her drool on his pillow. He would stare at her late into the night, studying her profile, her cat's eyes, drinking in every detail. The way her lips curled up to twist in a secret smile, and her eyebrows, lids and eyes. One eye was blue, and the other a light green. The secret codes, the lovers' language, the baby talk. He loved the poems they sent each other. She could actually wiggle her ears! He thought that was incredible. The way she smelled. He stroked her face with the back of his hand. Her hair was soft with a golden brown-red curl. Amazing. The way she danced around his place. She did her "puppy dog paws" begging impression. The way she chewed and nuzzled at his beard.

He loved her passion.

Deep into the night, they would caress each other and fiercely make love together. They watched movies in bed, drank wine and feasted.

(As they lay together, she would fidget and squirm with her legs like a cricket.)

The day they met, he stumbled as an idiot, stammering. He said,

"Don't I know you from somewhere? I've seen you about the town? Did you go to school with me? I love your hair, it's very striking!"

Her face reminded him of a poem he knew by Thomas Hardy; her whole demeanour did.

"Where you will next be there's no knowing,

Facing round about me everywhere,

With your nut-coloured hair,

And grey eyes, and rose-flush coming and going."

He was bright purple. She said,

"Thank you for that compliment!" She touched his shoulder and added, "You're my friend for life."

He asked her to coffee, and she agreed. Then lunch. One time, he was embarrassed to admit something to her, saying by text message,

"Would it freak you out to know that I pee into a bottle?"

She threw her head back and laughed. "No!" was her reply, and she just took his hand.

They became friends, even lovers. He was in a daydream; he thought he had everything going for him. She spoiled him and, in return, he spoiled her.

She would even sit on his knee and they drove around the town on his electric wheelchair. They giggled and laughed together. She said,

"If I was born in ancient times, I would be a Babylonian hedonist!"

And she was. She loved pleasure. She was a true wild child of nature.

They went everywhere together, did everything together, texted each other in synchronicity.

But he hated some of the music she liked to watch. He thought it was appalling nonsense. He didn't like the way she drank and smoked. She didn't like how he procrastinated and hesitated about decisions.

One time, on their travels, they met an elderly gentleman who was waiting for a train. He remarked about her golden red hair, saying,

"Red and green should never be seen together except on an Irish Queen!" She was wearing a green scarf.

They whispered to one another whilst they lay together. They would play word games, associations: she would say "moon," and he would say "star," and a chain would go on like that until dawn caught them. Together, as one.

"I love you very much, Gem Autumn, very much." She hugged him hard.

"I love you too, August Haws, very much."

At the very height of their relationship, she had done everything for him and he lapped it up like a greedy child. She put two new tyres on his wheelchair, toileted him, put him to bed whenever he wanted, made love to him. He made a present of an amber ring and matching earrings for friendship. She adored them.

One time, they met at the canal in early spring. They sat huddled together one Sunday in a hailstorm. She smoked four cigarettes as she talked about life and its consequences. The side of her nose transfixed him as the smoke seeped out and raced into the frozen air. The hail pelted their bags. She sheltered him with her umbrella, which was battered about in the fierce bitter wind.

A week earlier, they had sat in the graveyard and she had asked him to make a choice. That day was glorious: the heat shimmered over the gravestones.

"Wake up, my love," she glanced at the flowers she had taken and sat them on a gravestone. The stone had a simple single word they could discern and it was fading due to the time and ages. Her sister's name, but it wasn't a relative. She saw it one day in passing and, in respect, she honoured her name.

"Before we both go, we'll be a long time dead." An insect landed on her bag, and she did her dance to drive it away.

"Be your own man! Don't let anyone dictate to you." She lit up another cigarette. "And don't let me down. Honour me." She blew her smoke away and it spiralled up into the still air.

He was just blinded by the emotional tidal wave that was their friendship. He just nodded in agreement to everything that she said and did for him. He was spoiled —years of loneliness, the resulting aftermath of his parents dying, and himself almost dying. He was in shock and awe of this new world of hers.

A few months earlier, it happened, the schism. His sister came to visit, bringing food. The two women didn't see eye to eye. She thought his sister insulted her, and vice versa. He was burning a high fever and he could not distinguish what was happening. He delved into his mind to salvage the situation. He couldn't. Because of his brain jury, he was classed "incapacitated" and he tried to prove his independence. He talked to the wrong people, gained advice from inexperienced "professionals." She put a lot of pressure on him. His family became concerned and worried. Friends, too.

But he was blinded by love. And he thought he could do anything for her love. He couldn't. He folded into his family that had supported him all his life. His girlfriend was outraged by his behaviour. She lashed out at him in all ways. Hell hath no fury.

They had such dreams that lovers have. He supported her through a long cold winter, finding her employment through his Internet access. He found her two employers. In return, she gave him love.

The summer past was incredible for him. One very memorable night was

August thirteenth. The previous night, there was the annual meteor shower. Truly, that evening was the most romantic, sensual, sexual and entirely beautiful lovemaking of his life.

"Always remember this night," they vowed to one another. They made love by candlelight, everywhere in his apartment. She made love to him with feral intensity. Like an animal, she pounced and clawed, scratched him, and he did the same as best as he could. Their climax was hard and passionate and she climaxed three times, he twice. He looked at her necklace, the star and crescent moon, and thought about the shooting stars outside in the dark above. She saw seven meteors that night, and she wished upon them, for them both.

Spent, they slept in each other's arms.

But, their time together was spent fighting as much as lovemaking. She was fiery and passionate, and they were always at odds with one another's lifestyles. One evening, whilst they lay together, she scratched him like a vicious cat and he pulled her hair.

She pulled away. She started to cry.

In shock, he tried to comfort her, and console her. He was deeply ashamed of himself. He remembered too late what was done to her in the past; her childhood had been very traumatic.

From that incident on, combined with many other mistakes he made, everything was falling apart. She came back to him on numerous occasions. Each time, the pattern repeated itself. He would break down and so would she. Then, they would make love, fight, and make up. The very last time they had sex was so intense it was indescribable. They fought and yelled at each other, giving each other intense sex. Afterwards, she stormed out, leaving her earrings and ring behind her, throwing them away.

He was in utter turmoil and desperation. This was his first relationship breakdown, and he almost had a nervous breakdown. The pressure was too much for both of them.

He tried to kill himself.

His sister forced him to choose between his family and his girlfriend. His girlfriend wanted to take him on holiday to Disney World, Paris and even further to Japan to try out an experimental walking aid to help him walk again. He had a doctor's letter that gave him permission to travel. His sister crumpled it up and threw it away right in front of him. His mind went to a very dark place when she did that to him.

He just wanted to walk. Why didn't all of them see that? Why wouldn't they just leave him alone with his August? He yearned to run in the fields once more…

"The bringing of me here; nay, bring me here again!

I am just the same as when

Our days were a joy, and our paths through flowers."

That night, he attempted suicide, but his best friend came to see him. He told him he had too much to live for and achieve. His friend said,

"It's good to be alive."

Oh, God, yes. It is good to be alive.

Returning to the present, at the park, they went to watch the ducks. She sat on his lap, curling up into a ball, hugging him. They just sat and watched the ducklings frolic. He was numb. She had all the answers to everything, but he did not want to listen.

That was his problem: stubborn male pride.

They stopped at the path for a warm kiss and then proceeded on to the local café where they met for coffee almost every day. She said,

"My gem, do I have your permission to kiss another man? Because every time I go to kiss anyone else, I see your sad face staring up at me."

He laughed, "Non!" he said, speaking French. "It's copyright!"

Then, abruptly, she turned and left.

He called her name in the street, but she was gone.

"I was chained by fate. Chained by circumstances beyond my control. We all are. But one day, a woman came into my life and tried to set me free. She was so free, nothing stopped her from living her own life and, for a time, we were happy together. Then, one day, it changed for the worse for us both. I tried to be as independent as possible, but the chains of the past came back to haunt us both. The chains of sanity broke and I almost went over into the abyss. When people say they love you, they put a chain around your heart, and when it shatters, what are you left with? A cold and open door in your guts, soul and heart, and brutal, cruel freedom."

She said, "There are only a few things in life that are truly free: the wind in your hair, the stars, and a person's dreams."

Was it all just a dream? Is everything?

He found a corner to break down and cry uncontrollably. That night, he hugged her pillow. Remembering, always remembering that swing.

Always, August.